LEADERSHIP FOR OLDER ADULTS

D1508557

LEADERSHIP FOR OLDER ADULTS

Aging with Purpose and Passion

Sandra A. Cusack, Ph.D.
Wendy J. A. Thompson, M.A.

BRUNNER/MAZEL
Taylor & Francis Group

USA	Publishing Office:	BRUNNER/MAZEL *A member of the Taylor & Francis Group* 325 Chestnut Street Philadelphia, PA 19106 Tel: (215) 625-8900 Fax: (215) 625-2940
	Distribution Center:	BRUNNER/MAZEL *A member of the Taylor & Francis Group* 47 Runway Road Levitttown, PA 19057 Tel: (215) 269-0400 Fax: (215) 269-0363
UK		BRUNNER/MAZEL *A member of the Taylor & Francis Group* 1 Gunpowder Square London EC4A 3DE Tel: +44 171 583 0490 Fax: +44 171 583 0581

LEADERSHIP FOR OLDER ADULTS: Aging with Purpose and Passion

Copyright © 1999 Taylor & Francis. All rights reserved. Printed in the United States of America. Except as permitted under the United States Copyright Act of 1976, no part of this publication may be reproduced or distributed in any form or by any means, or stored in a database or retrieval system, without prior written permission of the publisher.

1 2 3 4 5 6 7 8 9 0

Printed by George H. Buchanan, Phila., PA 1998.

A CIP catalog record for this book is available from the British Library.
 ⊗ The paper in this publication meets the requirements of the ANSI Standard Z39.48-1984 (Permanence of Paper).

Library of Congress Cataloging-in-Publication Data is available from the publisher.

ISBN 0-87630-931-7 (PB)

DEDICATION

To the promise of a new old age. To a paradigm that takes us deep into the life experience of our elders, one that gives us new eyes with which to see and serve the higher needs—the desires and aspirations—of older adults.

CONTENTS

PREFACE

Whatever is old is new again. That was the message of the 1890s, as it was the message of the 1990s—but with a difference. The world is experiencing population aging at a dramatic rate. In the United States, the population over age 65 will more than double between now and 2050 (Bureau of the Census, 1995). The year 1999 was declared the International Year of Older Persons, and as we enter the 21st millennium, the challenge is to restore the natural order and give older people back their rightful place in history. Every older person is a leader by virtue of preceding all who follow through life and through time, and their rich experience can be our gain.

Our population is aging, society is aging, and our institutions are aging. The characteristics of older people are changing, however, and if aging institutions and organizations are to meet the exciting challenges this new age presents, we first need to consider what is really new about being old. We can then deconstruct and reconstruct aging organizations and institutions to meet the real needs of older people of today. And by *older* or *old* or *senior* or *elder* we mean anyone over the age of 50, because 50 is typically the age at which people become eligible to join many seniors' groups and organizations. Furthermore, according to British historian Peter Laslett, 50 has become a marker age at which people typically enter the third age or retirement phase of their lives. In America, many people seem to want to stop the clock at 50.

More than 20 years ago, Bernice Neugarten and others wrote compellingly of moving toward an "age-irrelevant" society. Have we arrived? We may have succeeded too well in creating such an age-irrelevant society, leaving people of every age without a clear sense of their own history and connectedness to the past and the future. We have in many ways succeeded in irradicating both old age and childhood from the life span. Are children little copies of adults? Two-year-olds have the latest hairstyles and wear grown-up clothes. Many adults are "lost in the 50s"—Ken Dychtwald calls it "middlescence"—and everyone over 50 strives to stay middle-aged forever. No one ever admits to being old. Why would they? To be old is to be of little value, to be discarded and no longer needed. Some older people say they are treated like deadwood. Why is it we value antiques, as long as they are neither alive nor resemble us?

In the 1970s, Robert Butler asked provocatively, "Why survive growing old in America?" In the 1980s, Harry Moody wrote of an "abundance of life" in old age. In the 1990s, human resource experts tell us investing in the human resource capital of an aging society makes good sense because older people represent the greatest proportion of able-bodied—and sound-minded—people. Furthermore, if they are not engaged, stimulated, and challenged, according to activity theorists, older people will become an even greater burden on the economy as they age. We pay lip service to this abundance of life, making little effort to discover the conditions under which older people do more than survive. At the end of the 20th century, Thomas Cole tells us that old age remains "a season in search of a purpose."

Disengagement theory, one of the most widely held gerontological theories for many decades, has left us with a legacy that we need to lay to rest. Clearly, no society can afford to promote and support a generation of people who are disengaged and noncontributing members. More to the point, people do not want to disengage from life at any age. Human development does not stop at 50, 65, 80, or 100; it goes on forever. And no one wants to be a dropout.

The reality is that we still equate retirement with old age and disengagement. In mandating retirement, we strip people of their status as full members of society when they still have 20 or 30 good years left. Paul Tournier (1988) paints a grim picture of the realities of retirement that result from equating retirement with old age and retiring people from life while they are still vital and alive:

> [There is] serious confusion between "retirement" and "old age," as if to retire were to signify being old! With the exception of a few very arduous professions that lead to premature aging, most workers are still in full possession of their physical, mental and social capacities on retirement. The proof of this is that they all had responsible jobs only the day before. The abrupt transition from being fully active to a state of total inactivity is completely contrary to the laws of Nature. (pp. 13, 14)

Tournier speaks of legions of retired people who are fit for work, feel like they have been scrapped, and suffer boredom and depression.

Yes, but that was the 1980s, you may say. Attitudes have changed. We know that older people today are healthier and more active than they were at any other period in history. Have our attitudes really changed? Or are we just replacing negative stereotypes with positive stereotypes while avoiding the real issues—like the experience of being silenced and feeling invisible expressed by the following people:

> As children we were taught to be seen and not heard. When we retire, the message society gives us is the same. Furthermore, we are told that we aren't needed any more. It's deja vu! We are back to where we started. Once again, the message is to be seen and not heard. And often our families reinforce that message.

> I experience loss of respect when I am shopping and a clerk passes me by to wait on someone younger. I feel like a nonperson. If people don't ask my opinion, I eventually withdraw and feel negative. People treat seniors like deadwood.

Most people derive a sense of self-worth and self-esteem from their work, and retirement consequently brings with it a loss of self-esteem. Older people, particularly women, speak freely of the loss of self-esteem that accompanies aging. Although men rarely articulate feelings of low self-esteem using those words, they often admit to feeling worthless or not needed. Unless retired people put their skills and talents to use in some productive way, the loss of self-esteem can have grave consequences for social, emotional, and physical health. The opportunity to play a voluntary leadership role can turn the loss of self-esteem around, as it did for one woman who said,

> I need to be needed. As the president of a seniors' center, I feel I am needed. I never wanted to retire from work, and I treat my volunteer responsibilities just like work. I give it all I've got. I gain satisfaction and increasing self-esteem as I go along . . . and what I have gained in volunteer work spills out into all the other areas of my life.

Not many people, however, have the opportunity to play such a challenging and fulfilling social role. More commonly, formal roles on advisory and executive boards are token appointments. Often boards of seniors are called advisory or executive "groups," suggesting that members of a group do not have the same legitimate power that the term *board* connotes. One retired professor, a member of the advisory board to a leadership development project, expressed gratitude when he said, "So much of the work that I am involved in is just token participation. It gives me a deep sense of satisfaction to be 'used' in the good sense of the term."

Helen Kerschner (1994) reports that both professionals and older Americans were surprised by themes that emerged from focus groups held across the United States before the 1995 White House Conference on Aging:

Among those that were somewhat surprising; being viewed negatively by the media, being excluded from decision and policy making, being isolated from society, being seen as unimportant "excess baggage." Other surprises are the high level of confidence that participants have about the important role they could play if society would only allow it, their very negative view toward younger people, and their perception of the negative view younger people have toward them. (p. 4)

Surprising? What is most surprising is that these seniors have a high level of confidence in what they have to offer, despite the ageist attitudes rampant in North America and the lack of opportunities for productive engagement and leadership. What is disturbing is the negative attitudes held by younger people toward elders and the negative view that older people have toward younger people. What has happened to the natural affinity of young and old? Tragically, the two groups are becoming adversaries in the competition for scarce resources, and policy makers often fuel the fire.

Those who are middle-aged or middlescent recall a natural order of life, a time of greater respect between the generations. Many remember their grandparents as people who were very old, yet played a central role in their lives, who instilled certain cultural values and beliefs, perhaps guiding them on particular career paths. The history of leadership in many other cultures reflects attitudes toward elders as wise spiritual leaders, which accord them a recognized place in society. That place in society also afforded them a measure of status. How have those positive attitudes come to be replaced by a pervasive attitude toward the elderly as unproductive and a burden on society?

The attitudes of youth reflect the dominant attitude of our youth-oriented society and the values of the marketplace. Historically, elders were valued as the transmitters of culture. In these postmodern times, traditional cultural values on which North America was founded have been replaced by pop culture and the mystique of technology. With a limited job market, the emphasis in public schooling and higher education is on making a living, rather than making a life. Postman (1995) states,

That the Technology God enslaves and gives no profound answers in the bargain is now increasingly well understood. We are left at last with no loom to weave a fabric to our lives . . . we need a story that will help us "to be people with an elementary sense of justice, the ability to see things as others do, a sense of transcendental responsibility, optimal wisdom, good taste, courage, compassion and faith." (p. 72)

This is the story that senior citizens have to tell anyone who is prepared to listen. Although older people may have little to teach today's youth about how to make a living in today's virtual reality, they have a great deal to say about another reality, about what is worth knowing and what is worth caring about. Negative attitudes about seniors as noncontributing, burdensome members of society can be changed to positive attitudes about seniors as productive participants who have unique contributions to make. Where and how do we begin? Instead of engaging youth to teach seniors how to operate computers, we can provide opportunities for elders to develop skills and confidence to take on leadership roles in groups and communities around the world.

The time has come to put human history back on course—to bury that old, outworn "use it or lose it" dictum. (Why, indeed, should anyone care if they lose it, if there is no real use for it in the first place?) Old people do not need to be stimulated and challenged because they will become a burden: they need it because they are human beings! Everyone, regardless of gender, race, or age, wants and needs to be a contributing member of society. And we need their contribution. Those who have survived the vicissitudes of life and times, having experienced world war and the great depression of the 1930s, may be the best equipped to guide us through the recessions and depressions of today and tomorrow. Those who know the meaning of community from a different age have much to teach those who follow and now rely on a sense of community for survival.

The trend toward empowering individuals and groups is occurring in organizations around the world (Thurz et al., 1995). Empowerment is most critical, however, in organizations that serve the needs of senior citizens, who are more accustomed to being consumers of service than partners in service delivery. How do those with a traditional organizational management perspective effectively shift a greater measure of responsibility and legitimate power to seniors, both individually and collectively? How do professionals shift from a service delivery orientation to one of working with a new breed of senior citizens who are enlightened and empowered? Traditional leadership no longer works in retirement organizations (if it ever did). No one wants to be told what to do, and retirement means they no longer have to take orders. With freedom of choice and no compelling options, people may choose to disengage. As a result, retirees lose the opportunity for rich engagement in later life, and society misses their contribution.

How do we make the changes that are necessary so that organizations reflect this new age and can respond to the real needs, desires, and capacities of older adults? We begin by giving older people a legitimate voice and listening to them in a new way: value their experience and their perspective; listen to their needs, dreams, and aspirations, achievements, and their strengths; and keep an ear to the ground for the muted voices, the assumptions seldom expressed, the ageist attitudes of decline and disengagement that serve as self-fulfilling prophecies. With a critical awareness of the way in which ageist attitudes permeate groups and organizations, choking the expression of talents and desires, we can then begin to change the structure of power and leadership, transforming organizations into self-renewing cultures of leadership.

This book tells the tale of two seniors' centers that reflect common leadership issues in retirement organizations throughout the Western world, issues that are just beginning to emerge in many developing countries (e.g., Africa and South America) and are yet to be experienced in others. Whatever the country where rapid population aging is coupled with a view of old people as useless and a burden, the challenge will continue to be one of how we develop the resources, the leadership potential, of our aging population. How do we turn old age from an expensive wasteland into a fertile period of growth and development of personal potential and maximum contribution to the community?

The centers showcased in Chapters 4 and 5 serve as case studies and the people as portraits of leadership in action, illustrating the influences on their development as leaders and highlighting common issues and variations within a theoretical framework. The first center, Carnegie Hall, is a model for what is possible in retirement organizations. Like De Pree's (1997) ideal for both profit and nonprofit organizations, it is a place of "realized potential." The second, Centennial Center, represents a more typical retirement organization, one that embodies a traditional authoritarian form of leadership. The challenge for this organization, like many of its kind around the world, is to transfom the leadership from an authoritarian model to an empowering one that focuses on developing the leadership potential of all its members. Like Charles Dickens' famous tale of two cities, this tale also reflects the spirit of liberté, egalité, and *fraternité* in a climate of change and democratization. Notions of democracy, however, go far beyond the dictatorship of the majority to encompass a true participatory democracy in which each voice is heard and every member of the community is a potential leader.

What we are talking about is fulfilling the American dream of equality for all people regardless of gender, race, *or age*. Feminism has a voice; multiculturalism is high on the political agenda. It is time to conquer the last deadly "ism." Ageism is insidious, subtle and pervasive, affecting not just senior citizens but all members of society. We must recognize it and eradicate it. No society can be healthy that fails to honor and respect its senior citizens, and no individual can be healthy who shrinks from the image of a future self.

Comes the revolution! It is time to translate the rhetoric of productive aging into reality. We can restore legitimate power to older people. We can commit ourselves to reforming and revitalizing aging institutions and organizations so that they serve the higher order needs of all people—notably the desire to develop their full human potential to the end of life and to contribute their unique skills and talents to their families, organizations, communities, and the world. Such is the promise and the possibility of this vital new old age. And such is the promise of this book.

The book is divided into three parts. Part I provides a theoretical perspective. Chapter 1 begins with an introduction to this new age and the leadership challenge it presents. Chapter 2 provides a closer look at leadership, what we know about leadership and about the culture of organizations, then focuses on leadership in the third age, or retirement phase, of life and what is different about seniors' organizations that requires a particular approach to leadership. As a prelude to organizational change, Chapter 3 provides the framework for understanding, exploring, and interpreting the culture of organizational leadership.

Part II contains the real-life stories of leaders and leadership in action. In Chapters 4 and 5, portraits of leadership in two centers are drawn; voices tell the stories, illuminating beliefs, values, and hidden assumptions concerning the nature of retirement, the needs and desires of seniors, and the nature of power and leadership. In Chapter 6, profiles of three leaders are drawn, including how they found their voice and how they found their feet.

Part III provides concrete instructions and practical tips for those transformational leaders who believe in the potential of the vast majority of older people to contribute substantively to community life and to play a leadership role. Chapter 7 describes the needed shift from power to empowerment in seniors' organizations and how to be the catalyst. In Chapter 8, the focus is personal leadership style and how to become a more empowering leader. The final chapter takes us back to the basics of leadership training, describing the kind of education and training that transforms people's lives in extraordinary ways.

This book was written for those dedicated professionals and voluntary leaders of all ages across America and around the world who work in a multitude of seniors' groups and organizations—managers and directors of seniors centers, public and nonprofit agencies serving seniors, nursing homes and adult day centers; members of executive boards and advisory groups; senior volunteers who serve peers, families, and communities as leaders and service providers. It is for anyone who shares our belief in the infinite possibilities of old age and wants to make a difference.

ACKNOWLEDGMENTS

Many people have supported this work from its inception to the final writing, and we thank you. We are particularly indebted to Joy Barkwill and Jill Rowledge, exemplary professional leaders, who share our belief in the leadership potential of older adults and provided invaluable personal insights from the professional's perspective.

We wish to thank all those seniors who have entrusted us with personal experience and who continue to enrich our lives. We also acknowledge the professional support of Gloria Gutman, Director of the Gerontology Research Centre, and Chair of the World Congress on Aging 2001, Simon Fraser University, Vancouver, British Columbia, Canada. We especially want to thank Dr. Mike Manley-Casimir, Professor in the Faculty of Education, Simon Fraser University, who is a true servant leader.

ACKNOWLEDGMENTS

INTRODUCTION TO LEADERSHIP FOR OLDER ADULTS

As a prelude to creating effective leadership in any organization, the first part of this book sets the stage. Chapter 1 outlines the leadership challenge of this new age, describes what is new about it, and elucidates why developing leadership is more important now than ever. Ageist attitudes and assumptions are presented that limit late life potential and serve as formidable barriers to the emergence of seniors as leaders. Chapter 2 offers a historical perspective on leadership research and theory, insights into leadership skills and styles, and an approach to leadership that works most effectively in retirement organizations. To facilitate the emergence of effective leadership, one must begin with a deep understanding of the organization—how leadership currently works, who has the power, how is it shared, and, most important, what are the nonproductive attitudes and assumptions about leadership that are barriers to be overcome? A framework for understanding organizational culture is outlined in Chapter 3.

CHAPTER 1

Leadership Challenge of a New Age

To recapture spirit, we need to relearn how to lead with soul. How to breathe new zest and buoyancy into life. Leading with soul returns us to ancient spiritual basics—reclaiming the enduring human capacity that gives our lives passion and purpose.

—Bolman & Deal, 1995, p. 6

☐ This New Age

The time has come to review and renew the meaning of old age. During the 20th century, medical science has succeeded in extending the human life span by more than 20 years, but in many ways society has failed to ascribe a legitimate social function to those added years. In the 1960s and 1970s, social demographers ominously predicted the graying of America. Viewing older people generally as disengaged, dependent, noncontributing members of society, they forewarned of the inevitable increase in society's burden of caring for catastrophic numbers of elderly people. Gerontology was developed and established as a science and a profession.

The predicted burgeoning of the aging population is becoming a fact of life around the world. With a membership of 33 million people, the American Association of Retired People (AARP) is the single largest voluntary organization in the United States (Pratt, 1995). Since its inception in 1986 with a membership of 16 people, the Canadian Association of Retired People (CARP) has grown at an astonishing rate, unmatched by any other Canadian association (CARP membership topped 300,000 in 1997). And organizations representing older people are growing in many parts of the world. Vitez estimated in 1997 that "in 25 years, in nearly every country in the Northern Hemisphere—Russia, China, all of Europe, the United States, and Canada—one in every five people will be older that sixty" (p. 1). Dr. Robert Butler of the NIA says, "We haven't found any biological reason not to live to 110. . . . This added lifespan is not just extra time to kill; it represents potentially vital, productive years in which older people can either contribute to their society or drain its resources" (Vitez, 1997, p. 1)

In America, life expectancy has increased by 28 years from an average of 47 years in 1900 to 75.5 and 78.9 for women in the 1990s. The change in life expectancy in this century is greater than the change in life expectancy during the previous 2000 years (Lamdin & Frugate, 1997). The numbers aren't surprising, but the people often are. No one anticipated or prepared for the emerging face of old age.

While the numbers were growing, a second and much quieter revolution was taking place. The face of age was changing—a new breed of *Homo sapiens* was emerging. Those who really came to know them individually found that older people were much more than they anticipated. Anyone who really listened to their stories marveled at their courage, their creativity, their passion, their deep understanding of human nature and the meaning of life. Older people who were "ordinary"—neither wealthy nor elite and often uneducated—seemed somehow exceptional and extraordinary.

Long-held attitudes and assumptions about old age and old people linger, left over from a reality that no longer exists. Blinded by ageist expectations, people fail to see the richness and diversity of older people and seldom nurture the infinite possibilities they present. No wonder so many retirees talk about feeling "invisible": no one sees them as people, but as old people. In other words, the mask of old age renders the real person invisible.

Not only do the ageist stereotypes die hard, they serve as self-fulfilling prophecies for most older people. People learn how to grow old by watching others grow old, severely limiting the possibilities for growth and productivity. The challenge is to reconstruct the meaning of old age, to view the aging of society as the unprecedented triumph that it is, and to envision possibilities for growth and productivity unprecedented and unrecorded in human history. As the younger generation would say, it is time to do a reality check and get an attitude. Not an easy task.

A New Old Age

The subject of old age has always been fraught with ambivalence. Most people have compassion for old people but shrink from the image of an aging self. Everyone loves "grandma," but few aspire to be like her.

Ageism is insidious in many societies, subtle and pervasive, affecting not just senior citizens but all members of society. Yet rarely is it recognized and addressed. Getting beyond simple negative or positive stereotypes requires a fundamental shift from viewing older people as the problem, to seeing them as those most capable of helping younger generations to understand *real* problems and develop creative solutions.

What are these dramatic changes in society? What are the most salient characteristics of older people today? What are the most pressing needs of society? And what are the needs of older people? Who should be served first—people or society? Must we always choose? There is a better way to serve the real needs (i.e., the desires and aspirations) of this new breed of older person and in the process to serve the most pressing needs of a changing society. First, the reality check. Let's begin with what, on the surface, appears to be the good news.

The Good News

The mass aging of our society (and others throughout the world) may well be the most extraordinary evolutionary event of all time. During 99% of the time that humans have walked this planet, average life expectancy has been under 18 years. We have never before had a mass population of older people. Until very recently, most people did not age, they died relatively young. During the past century something tsunamic began. As a result of dramatic advances, most of us will age. We are witnessing the birth of a 21st century "gerontocracy" (Dychtwald, 1997, p. 11).

In his address to the American Society on Aging (1994), Dychtwald characterized the changes and challenges in many ways. He described social reality in terms of changing social policy:

- New directions in healthcare policy, increasing emphasis on health promotion.
- Reduced social services, increasing role of the caregiver.

He described the most salient characteristics of the aging population as follows:

- The number of older people has increased, and the proportion of women is higher.

- Older people are healthier and better educated.
- The wealthiest people are over 50 years of age, and money is no problem.
- The baby boomers turn 50 in 1996, and no one wants to grow old.

This is Dychwald's reality, and these are the challenges. The growing population of healthier and better educated older people (most of them women) will require opportunities for higher education and involvement in volunteer roles and work opportunities when family responsibilities diminish. Because of reduced healthcare and social service entitlements, everyone must assume greater responsibility for their own health and for providing social support and care to others. This group generally has the money and the education to take care of their own needs, and because many do not want to grow old, they will seek high-tech options to help them stay young forever.

Dychtwald further suggests that aging must be viewed as a continuum. The four boxes of life—you learn, you work, you rest, you die—no longer apply. People will need to retrain and retool at any age, and they will need opportunities for self-expression and enjoyment at any age. However, the danger in viewing aging as a continuum is that it implies a maintenance of the status quo, with no possibility for evolution or progression. Age seems irrelevant except as something to be overcome. And given that the wealthiest people are over 50 years of age and money is no problem, the current cohort of older adults would seem to have the means and re-sources to overcome their own aging. The hidden assumption and the political agenda in many developed and developing countries around the world is that they will also assume society's burden of caring, economi-cally and in kind, for the even more dramatically growing number of frail elderly people.

The good news reflects a new positive stereotype of aging—the glossy tabloid image that serves no one's best interests in the long run. Herein lies the rationale for reducing subsidies and entitlements for health, edu-cation, and social services for senior citizens. In both the United States and Canada, entitlements and subsidies have come increasingly under attack.

The Bad News: Issues of Entitlement and the Erosion of Subsidies

Butler suggests that

> we're in an extraordinarily uncomfortable, even mean-spirited period of our history. The social protections we have are beginning to be frayed, and we are seeing extraordinary and harsh attacks upon children, unwed

mothers, women, especially older women. (as cited in *Aging Today*, 1995, p. 4)

To suggest that the wealthiest people in America are more than 50 years old is no rationale for the removal of entitlements. The wealthiest people have always been over 50, and today is no exception. Furthermore, this group is anomalous, and developing social policy based on an anomalous generation will certainly have dire consequences for future generations, who will be less affluent. More to the point, people who are over 50 are rarely wealthy. Money is a problem for many older people, particularly older women who, despite their marginality and vulnerability, are expected to assume an even greater share of family caregiving responsibilities than they have in the past.

These can be dangerous times, when benevolent entitlements and subsidies to minority groups and seniors are being minimized through "clawbacks." Entitlements and subsidies to seniors are increasingly targeted and blamed for the deficit and are further jeopardized by the general view that older adults are wealthy. In the *Bulletin of the AARP*, Carlson (1994) warns, "Older Americans may see the 'wide-spread support' for Social Security in America begin to erode. Entitlement programs have been unfairly blamed for our nation's deficit." (p. 4). Headlines in a 1995 newspaper of the American Society on Aging (Retsinas) were also ominous: "Clouds gather over social security." The newspaper elaborated,

> The optimism of only one year ago had dissipated. . . Although the several hundred experts—economists, actuaries, political scientists and government bureaucrats—seemed to agree that the sky is not falling, they were concerned that clouds now blot the horizon. (p. 1)

Meanwhile, the same dark clouds were drifting over senior citizens north of the border. The headlines in the newsletter of CARP (1994) read, "[Federal government] chipping at the age tax credit" and went on to warn,

> Increasingly, seniors who have provided for their own retirement are being made to pay a larger share of the government's fiscal shortfall, whether by pension clawbacks, cutbacks in health and other services, or selective tax increases—and this is a trend that is bound to continue because the deficit problem is far from over. (p. 14)

And this ethos is being played out in various ways throughout communities across the country. The coordinator of a seniors' center speaks of a prevailing ideology that can be felt in his community:

> Often an idea starts in the business community, then translates into the public sector. A local hardware store has recently taken away reduced rates

for seniors, and the public sector has begun to remove subsidies for seniors. There is a myth that says seniors have lots of money and they don't need subsidies for recreation and education.

The trend toward cutting subsidies, eliminating staff, and severely reducing grant opportunities to seniors groups and organizations is widespread.

Canadian social gerontologist Ellen Gee summarized the demographics of an aging society as consisting of two realities reflecting the two faces of aging: (1) increasing numbers of people in the over-85 group, resulting in the increased burden of care, and (2) increasing numbers of healthy, able older adults (Gee & Gutman, 1995). She challenges policymakers to resist reductionist policies that pit seniors and younger people against each other in the competition for scarce resources. She recommends a more proactive approach to reintegrating older people into the wider society. What is needed is a change in attitude toward older people and their productive capabilities and a change in the attitudes and values of older people themselves, many of whom have come to view early retirement—that is disengagement or early departure from the workplace—as a right. She concludes that

> we will fare better in our attempts to mesh social policy and population aging if we focus our attention on [issues of empowerment], and cease attempts to either tinker with existing policies or challenge fundamental principles of the social welfare state as it has developed in the Canadian case. (p. 26)

In times of economic recession and restraint, everyone, regardless of race, gender, or age, has fewer rights and more responsibilities. The message is loud and clear: there is no free lunch and there are no free rides. This message has particular implications for seniors. The focus must be on developing services to enable people to stay in their own communities and in control of their own lives, and to continue to be productive (Gee & Gutman, 1995; *Aging Today*, 1995). If seniors who are able and healthy are expected to assume the major burden of caring for increasing numbers of socially disadvantaged persons who are no longer served by professionals, focusing on what will enable them to assume that responsibility is critical. The empowerment of senior citizens, individually and collectively, is the first priority. What kinds of professional support, what kinds of organizational structures, and what styles of leadership will facilitate the emergence of seniors as trained community leaders?

☐ Empowerment

The trend toward empowering individuals and groups is worldwide. As the population ages, communities are relying more on informal, voluntary networks of support to assist in the delivery of needed social services to seniors. The growing population of able seniors is an abundant resource deserving every opportunity for training and support. A central mandate of social services across America is to empower seniors—to give them greater control over their personal lives and a larger role in decision-making processes in community groups and other organizations to which they belong. There is, however, little research or theory to guide professionals in transferring power and control and in enabling seniors to assume leadership roles. To simply step aside and let seniors run things themselves is naive and irresponsible, and fails to recognize the organizational structure and changing political context within which seniors and professionals work.

Ageing International, the journal of the International Federation on Aging, devoted an entire volume to the subject of empowering seniors around the world (Thurz, 1993). In making his case for empowerment, Daniel Thurz, President of the US National Council on Aging, noted that compassion and services are essential responses to an aging population. However, failure to go beyond a compassionate service-delivery approach often robs people of dignity and independence. Something more is needed—"personal and group power" (p. 2). The challenge Thurz issued to those who work in the field of aging throughout the world is to make the empowerment of senior citizens a priority.Why is it so important?

Empowering seniors is important because growing older is generally a disempowering process. Societal changes in response to aging can lead to a lack of power in a previously independent individual. Typically, the interaction of societal and individual factors in later life triggers a negative cycle of disempowerment, resulting in a need to reverse the cycle through "re-empowerment." Myers (1993) stated the issue clearly:

> The challenge for societies is to develop roles for older persons in which they can achieve a sense of meaning and purpose, which are respected by others, and which offer an effective barrier against the current vulnerability that exists for many older people. (p. 6)

Retirement is no longer a time of disengagement from community life, but a time of active engagement in challenging and worthwhile activities that can benefit both self and society. The first step is personal empowerment.

When I'm Fully in Charge of Me

When I'm fully in charge of me,
I can let you, too, be free.

When I am using fullest potential,
I can help others do the same.

When I am empowered and strong and sure,
I feel neither envious nor threatened.

When I can grow at my own rate,
I do not fear your taking anything away.

I do not fear your overtaking me.
—Natasha Josefowitz, 1983, p. 66

□ The Changing Nature of Retirement

Viewing retirement as an opportunity for growth and personal development represents a radical departure from traditions of research in aging
and retirement. The occurrence of a postwork or retirement phase of life
is a modern phenomenon. Three sociocultural theories of aging have
dominated the literature on activities of later life since the 1960s: disengagement theory, activity theory, and continuity theory. Disengagement
theory, associated with the work of Cumming and Henry (1961), supports
the notion of retirement as a process of disengagement from society and
increasing preoccupation with self. In opposition to disengagement theory, Havighurst (1963) suggested that the development of new social
roles to replace those from which the person has disengaged was important for successful aging, and this theoretical position became known
as activity theory. The third position, associated with Atchley (1972) and
Neugarten (1977), supports a life span perspective on aging and emphasizes the notion of continuity of activities, interactions, and responses.

   Streib and Schneider (1971) rejected disengagement theory because of
its pessimistic view of late life potential, and they rejected activity theory
because of its middle-class, middle-aged bias and the emphasis on keeping
busy. They suggested an adaptation of continuity theory that recognizes
the need to remain fully engaged in life, while taking into consideration

that new social roles for older people must reflect the normal losses and limitations of later life. More than merely busy work, social roles and activities "should be satisfying in social psychological terms and they must be recognized as valid pursuits that are prestigeful or socially useful by other members of society, old and young" (p. 181). The involvement in what Streib and Schneider called "citizenship-service" roles brings a new kind of usefulness and valued contribution to society in later life. That message, nearly 30 years ago, takes on new significance given the increasing numbers of healthier and more educated retirees and society's growing need for their contribution.

Retirement is being reconsidered and redefined in the western world (Gee & Gutman, 1995). The term itself conjures up negative connotations of disengagement, and some would suggest it is a concept that is no longer useful. With variability of the age of retirement and different experiences of men and women, the terms *senior* and *retirement* are both becoming less useful in considering trends and activities during later life. Describing individuals as being in the *third age* represents an alternative to the terms *elderly* and *senior* and a movement toward more respectful and adventurous labels.

The concept of the third age has both an individual and a collective definition (Laslett, 1987). A society in the third age is defined demographically as one in which 10% or more of the population is over 65 years of age and 50% of the adults over 25 can expect to live to at least 70—that is, the society must have both a measure of affluence and a larger number of people over 65. According to Laslett's criteria, Great Britain entered the third age in the 1950s and there are now more than 16 countries that share this status. The United States entered the third age in the 1970s, and Canada entered the third age in the early 1980s (National Advisory Council, 1988).

At the individual level, the third age can be conceived as the third of four stages in a life course (not marked by years). Laslett (1987) identified four developmental stages:

1. A stage of dependence, education, socialization
2. A stage of individualization and responsibility
3. A stage of personal achievement and fulfillment
4. A stage of dependence and decrepitude

Although many professionals experience a sense of personal achievement and fulfillment throughout their working lives (i.e., to some extent combining the second and third phases), it is the third stage that Laslett suggests is most characteristic of retirement.

The third age typically occurs, although not necessarily, after retirement from the workforce for men. With the increasing flexibility of the retirement age and options for work and leisure, it may conceivably be a temporary stage between employment, and it may also concur with part-time employment or a semiretired status. For women who have been homemakers, it may come after release from family responsibilities (e.g., after the death of a spouse or elderly parents). For both men and women, then, it is the period in later life characterized by active participation in self-chosen activities before the onset of dependency, should it occur. The promise of this new old age is that with productive and meaningful engagement in the third age, the period of decline and dependency—the fourth age—will be severely reduced or completely eliminated for most people.

☐ Changing Needs and Capacities of Retirees

The third age, or retirement stage, of life is increasingly accepted as a period of personal growth and active engagement in challenging and worthwhile enterprises. One of the needs of retired persons is to make a meaningful contribution. Although opportunities exist for retired professionals to serve their communities, little is known about the desires and expectations of the larger population of educationally less-advantaged people who have spent much of their working lives as clerks, technicians, laborers, homemakers, and so forth (Morris & Bass, 1986). This growing group of increasingly healthy and better educated retirees with a diversity of experience and life skills has great potential for social contribution. Critical to working with seniors and promoting their contribution is the development of a deep understanding of their needs, desires, and expectations.

What are the needs and expectations of the majority of able retired persons that affect their willingness to take on leadership roles in their groups and organizations? For many, retirement may be the first time that considerable choice is available (e.g., after the death of a spouse or release from a demanding job). Free from the daily demands of family or career responsibilities and the need to earn a living, many older adults may expect to play a little golf or bingo, to travel, or simply to relax. What factors might influence the choice to commit time to volunteer work in the community after many years of family or work-related responsibilities?

The most widely known and relevant work in understanding human motivation is that of Abraham Maslow, who outlines a hierarchy of needs that drive human behavior. According to Maslow (1968), there are five hierarchically organized levels of basic need: (1) physical needs (e.g., food, shelter); (2) the need for safety and security; (3) the social need for a sense of belonging, acceptance, and affection; (4) the ego's need for self-esteem, self-confidence, respect, and recognition; and, ultimately (5) the need for self-actualization, challenge, and fulfillment. (Maslow will be reconsidered in more detail throughout the book.)

Laslett's (1987) characterization of the third age suggests that retirement may well be the age of self-actualization, challenge, and fulfillment. If basic needs have been met for a significant portion of retired people in third-age societies, they may be motivated to take on leadership roles to satisfy their need for challenge, self-actualization, and fulfillment, as well as to gain or maintain a level of confidence, self-esteem, and recognition. As one woman in her 70s, a participant in a leadership training program, observed,

> When my husband retired, he sat around for a whole year. Then I got him to join the seniors' center and they gave him an important job where he was able to use his experience in business. He helped others and in doing it, helped himself. It was so good for his self-esteem. Maslow's hierarchy really does apply to retirement. It can be a time in your life when you really give generously to others.

People in retirement are motivated by a strong need to maintain a sense of personal control over their lives, and they choose activities and assume new roles that help them maintain the same level of power they experienced in their earlier years. Because older adults commonly experience a loss of power, the notion of power deserves particular attention. Does everyone who is retired need to maintain the same level of power over others that they experienced in their working lives? Or is it the level of personal power and control over one's own life that is important to a sense of well-being in later years? (George, the past president who will be introduced in Chapter 5, certainly seemed to have a need for power over others.) And what are the attitudes and assumptions about power that might cause one person to seek a measure of power and status through a voluntary leadership role and another to avoid it?

Traditionally, volunteer organizations have been the domain of the more privileged group in society—the professional's wife who had the luxury of time and money and who was unfulfilled as a wife and mother, or the doctor's wife who ran the hospital auxiliary. People with status and wealth generally gave freely of their time to those less fortunate; it was a way of paying back society for the privileged position they enjoyed. It offered a challenge and was a source of recognition and respect. The more education people had, the more they were inclined to volunteer.

Today, volunteerism takes on greater significance. As social services are being withdrawn, volunteers are needed to replace professional services to people of all ages who require them. As Theresa, who will be introduced in Chapter 5, observed, "Right now we are experiencing so many cutbacks in social services, not just to seniors but to all age groups. Volunteers have to take up the slack. How do we inform people that we need them to take the place of people who used to be paid?" Despite the fact that volunteerism has been recognized for some time as a way to replace the loss of a work role, seniors as a group are underrepresented in volunteer programs across the country. In this age of social transformation, seniors have a vital role to play as volunteers.

☐ Volunteerism in the Age of Social Transformation

The current period of history has been called the age of social transformation. Drucker (1994) writes of the decline of the industrial age and the emergence of the knowledge society, characterized by a proliferation of nonprofit organizations that have their own system of knowledge. He speaks of the development of "knowledges" rather than "knowledge" and claims that knowledge that is of value must be attached to an organizational context. The growth of the nonprofit (voluntary) sector provides the opportunity for both unpaid and paid employment. Volunteerism will have to be a way of life for everyone. To meet the needs of society in the future, much of the work will be done in the context of nonprofit organizations and everyone will have to contribute voluntarily. Everyone will have to "share or suffer." Giving time freely through volunteering will replace the dying market relationships in which people sell their time to others. Rifkin suggests that

> caring tasks could become the high-status jobs of the future. In a world where even highly technical jobs can be automated, "the kind of nurturing and community-building skills that characterize work in the volunteer sector are the least vulnerable to replacement by computers, robots and telecommunications technology." (as cited in *The Province*, 1995, p. A18)

Seniors are involved in a variety of both formal and informal volunteer roles in their families and church groups, in libraries and hospitals, and in the larger community. Informally, many are providing care to aged parents and ailing spouses, assisting with the care of grandchildren, and housing their adult children who are returning to the "cluttered nest" as a result of divorce, unemployment, or the high cost of housing (Mitchell & Gee, 1996). Many serve on boards and committees of retirement associations that provide an increasing array of social and educational services to members.

It seems society needs the contribution of seniors and they need to make it. People who have been conditioned over a lifetime to retire from public life at age 65, people who have served their families for 30 years, are now needed to become committed and involved in seniors' groups and to continue to serve the community. People who have never considered themselves to be leaders are being asked to assume leadership roles.

☐ The Challenge: Developing Seniors as Leaders

Despite the belief that retired people want and need to make a meaningful contribution to society, there is a severe shortage of people willing to share the leadership in their groups, organizations, and community centers. When the study of Centennial Center began, a sign in a prominent location at the center said, "Volunteers *desperately* needed." And that same sense of desperation was expressed over and over in surveys and discussions with seniors and professionals representing various seniors groups and organizations in the greater Vancouver area, throughout the province of British Columbia (which has more than 1,650 seniors groups), and across Canada. The most common leadership problem was getting both new and old members involved and willing to share the workload (Cusack et al., 1991). Little has changed and the demand is still growing.

Given the many reasons why retired people may want to commit themselves to productive roles, why do people express so much difficulty in getting seniors more involved? Many factors within an organization (e.g., people, personalities, circumstances, relationships, opportunities) effect whether seniors commit themselves to programs and activities. Of fundamental importance are the organization's recognition of the abilities of seniors and its willingness to use these talents. Seniors, however, need confidence in their abilities, a willingness to share experience and knowledge, and a willingness to take on responsible roles.

The opportunity to participate in a leadership training program can help seniors develop the essential leadership skills and confidence in their ability to contribute, but what about the attitudes of those professional leaders with whom they work? Negative attitudes toward old age and stereotypical perceptions of older people as less able, out of touch, forgetful, rigid, passive, and unwilling to make a commitment persist despite growing evidence to the contrary. These common views have an insidious effect on senior participation. In many cases, seniors say they want to feel useful, but they often experience a sense of tokenism regarding their participation in decision-making groups and processes. To what extent do organizations fully recognize and make use of the experience and abilities of older people? Ageist attitudes, both negative and positive stereotypes, that are held by the broader community and internalized by seniors serve as the greatest barriers to voluntary participation and leadership.

☐ The Biggest Barrier—Ageism

Ageism is a global concern, manifesting in different ways in different cultures. In Great Britain, for example, most people have difficulty being honest about attitudes toward old age and old people. Feelings not openly expressed manifest in subtle ways: "We give them crackers to pull at parties and deny them the right to take responsibility for their sexuality, their behavior, and their risk taking" (Alison Norman, 1987, p. 9). A study of social work practice in Scotland suggested social services to seniors were becoming rationed. Social workers believed that "elderly people, as compared with children, have had their lives and have no future contribution to make to society, so why bother with them?" (p. 10)

Attitudes and Assumptions That Limit Late Life Potential

Just as society is beginning to recognize that older people have much to contribute, "positive ageism" may be as limiting as the negative attitudes of the past. Bell (1992) explored the images of the elderly portrayed on television suggesting that older people were powerful, affluent, physically and socially active, smart, admired by others, sexually attractive but not sexually active, and not dealing with real problems of life. These findings were contrasted with characterizations of older adults before the 1980s as rarely smart, attractive, active, or sexy. These images are too good to be true and may have an eventual negative influence on viewers' understanding of older adults. Positive ageism will become even more important as communities around the world are faced with more older people and more costly programs for seniors only.

Erdman Palmore has studied ageism for more than three decades and is particularly concerned about positive ageism. Positive ageism reflects the notion that older people have a greater supply of the following (Palmore, 1990):

- Kindness—For which there is no support.
- Wisdom—For which there is no support.
- Affluence—Which is simply not true: 12% are below the poverty line.
- Eternal youth—For which there is no support.
- Happiness—There is a myth of serenity.
- Dependability—For which there is legitimate support.
- Political power—To the contrary, people lose power when they retire.
- Freedom—Many experience a greater element of choice and freedom. However, increased family care giving responsibilities and health or financial problems can severely limit personal freedom.

In particular, assumptions that older people generally have political power and freedom warrant further consideration.

This kind of "tabloid thinking" suggests all old people are well off, in good health, and able to take care of themselves. This pie in the sky attitude was previously ignored, but positive ageism is becoming as great a problem as negative ageism, because it leads to a number of negative consequences for individuals and society.

Consequences of Ageism

North American society will continue to reap the negative consequences of both positive and negative ageism until every citizen has legitimate opportunities for personal development and productive engagement well beyond the current age of retirement. Currently, there are economic costs to older people in the form of unprecedented budget cuts and the focus on dollars spent on income support, health, and welfare. There is political concern that income assistance, health, and pensions will be cut further. The personal costs include demoralization, loss of self-esteem, loss of function, and physical and mental decline. These result both from negative and positive stereotypes, because stereotypes simply do not address the realities.

The greatest economic cost comes from ignoring the productive and creative abilities of millions of older people who retire because they are age 65, a waste that is becoming greater as the baby boomers approach retirement. Palmore (1990) states,

> There are social and cultural costs of ignoring the wisdom and social support and cultural resources that are available for the elders in our country. Most traditional societies still use these resources and many social problems of industrialized societies (e.g., lack of adequate child care, juvenile delinquency, high crime, labor shortages) may be due to our neglect of these elder resources. (p. 7)

By ignoring what Friedan (1994) calls the "fountain of age," negative stereotypes about older people as less able and less productive are perpetuated, leading to age segregation and a lack of respect between young and old.

A Child's View of a Mobile Home Retirement Park

After Easter break, the teacher asked her small pupils how they spent their Easter holiday. One little boy's reply went like this:

We always spend Easter with Grandma and Grandpa. They used to live up here in a big brick house, but Grandma got retarded and they moved to Arizona. They live in a park with a lot of other retarded people. They all live in tin huts. They ride tricycles that are too big for me. They all go to a building they call the wrecked hall, but it is fixed now. They all do exercises, but not very well. There is a swimming pool, but I guess nobody teaches them, because they just stand there in the water with their hats on. My Grandma used to bake cookies for me, but nobody cooks there. They all go to restaurants that are fast and have discounts. When you come into the park, there is a dollhouse with a man sitting in it. He watches them all day, so they can't get out without him seeing them. I guess everybody forgets who they are, because they all wear badges with their names on them. I wish they would move back home. I guess the man in the dollhouse won't let them out.

unknown

Storm the gates! The time has come to rescue all grandmas and grandpas from retirement parks and age-segregated ghettoes around the world. It is time to declare war on the negative stereotypes of aging and reduced expectations of the aged that stunt their growth as persons and their ability to contribute as vital and productive members of society.

☐ The Possibilities of Age

Old age is a social construction. Creating and promoting stereotypes limits the possibilities for individual growth and self-expression. The youth trap perpetuates denial of the realities, preventing older people from achieving what is possibile. To realize the possibilities requires a deeper understanding of what people actually experience as they grow older. And a critical awareness is needed of how much of what people experience and are able to achieve is imposed by society's views and how much is limited by their own small expectations. As Friedan (1994) suggests, there are some important questions society must ask:

What further reaches of human growth can we envision? And what public policies in health care, housing, education, in labor, industry, church and synagogue, and government might nourish the emergence and societal use of these new dimensions in human vitality? (p. 31)

Older people, like the young, have bought into the negative image of old age. For some, that image serves as a self-fulfilling prophecy. Those who reject it assume that they are exceptions to the rule. Thus, the myth is perpetuated, and continued involvement in life is denied by the compassionate problem of the age mystique. Friedman further considers,

What are we doing by denying age? The more we seek the fountain of perpetual youth and go on denying age, defining age as problem, that problem will only get worse. For we will never know what we could be, and we will not organize in our maturity to break through the barriers that keep us from using our evolving gifts in society, or demand the structures we need to nourish them. (p. 68)

The vision of every retiree as a potential leader, as having a valuable and unique contribution to make, requires those who work with seniors to critically examine their personal attitudes toward older people and to consider the kind of climate and organizational structures that foster the creative expression of their talents. What is needed is to uncover and remove the barriers that prevent people from using their talents and skills. In particular, those who serve seniors—whether in paid or voluntary roles—must develop a sensitivity to ageist attitudes and assumptions within organizations and understand how to replace them.

Old attitudes and assumptions that serve as barriers include the following:

- *Attitudes about the nature of retirement* as either a time to disengage from society and just relax or a time to engage in frivolous activities or recover lost youth
- *Assumptions about the characteristics of seniors* as either healthy, wealthy, wise, sexy, youthful, and able to take care of themselves or lacking energy, often sick, generally passive and needing direction, and set in their ways. In both cases, the general attitude is that seniors are noncontributing members and a burden on society
- *Assumptions about the nature of leadership* as something that requires total commitment and dedication. Leaders are born, and most people will always be followers
- *Attitudes about the nature of power* as something few older people want and something a few seniors, notably an elite group of wealthy and powerful men, have in too great abundance.

These attitudes create formidable barriers to emergent leadership.

□   Why Study Seniors' Centers?

Seniors' centers are the focus for leisure activities for many older adults in retirement, and they are increasingly recognized as a critical link in the network of formal community care (Krout, 1986). In Carnegie Hall, the center described in Chapter 4, approximately 15% of the population in the community who are retired are active members of the center. Seniors serve as peer counselors, members of the executive board, volunteers in hot lunch programs, receptionists, hosts, and chairpersons of activity groups (e.g., bowling, woodworking, dancing, hiking, lifelong learning). This center, like many of its kind across North America and abroad, relies heavily on the willingness of seniors to take on leadership responsibilities.

In both the United States and Canada, seniors' centers are an ideal location within which to develop community outreach and support services, such as peer counseling programs and widows' support groups. Seniors' centers offer a wide range of opportunities for participation and leadership within an organizational structure that has a work orientation yet is nonthreatening and supportive of involvement and that confers peer status. (Payne, 1977) Participants are generally retired, healthy, and active, and many are looking for new interests and opportunities for personal development. Seniors' centers are a reservoir of talent. Chetkow-Yanoov (1986), based on studies of retired professionals in Israel, claimed,

> The prospect can be further enhanced if we invest in leadership-training programs as part of preparations for the creative use of leisure-time during the post-work years. The pool of potential time, energy, skills, and experience—appropriately distributed throughout voluntary and public community settings—might well be the focus of our efforts in the coming years. (p. 73)

Many agencies and organizations are incorporating volunteer positions and programs for the elderly that are designed to capitalize on the skills and resources developed over a lifetime. Visiting programs for frail elderly persons draw on the sensitivity and knowledge of retirees who serve both as visitors and as trainers of high school students involved in visiting programs. Mentoring programs involve older adults in tutoring youth with learning disabilities, which draws on their patience, compassion, and knowledge of children. Of particular importance to an aging community is the development of seniors' community centers offering recreational, educational, and social support services; these centers typically rely on senior volunteers for both program maintenance and leadership functions. Seniors' centers, because of their strategic location and their mandates, are in a position to transform an entire generation of retired people. Clarisse, a member of Centennial Center reflected,

> When I joined the center, I had a real need. I had been widowed and was grieving, and this place saved my life. Some people who are brought to the center by their kids have really been pushed around. They are waiting to die. They are afraid and meek—and they join groups and pretty soon they are teaching others. Getting involved and helping others keeps people from being sick. If people are busy, they don't get sick.

Seniors centers are the ideal environment within which to promote the development of seniors as leaders for all of the following reasons:

1   Centers offer a safe, comfortable environment for seniors.
2.   The mandate is "re-creation" and socialization.
3.   Emphasis is on health, leisure, activity, and lifelong learning.
4.   Location is usually central to other community services.
5.   When other services are withdrawn, seniors' centers pick up the slack.
6.   Many community self-help groups (e.g., for arthritis or Alzheimer's disease) hold their meetings in seniors' centers.
7.   Membership is generally large and diverse.
8.   Centers offer opportunities for people to build and display a range of talents.
9.   As the educational level rises, education is increasingly a part of the programming.
10.   Legitimate opportunities exist for seniors to participate in decision-making processes (e.g., to serve as leaders).
11.   Service delivery increasingly depends on effective senior leadership.
12.   Many seniors spend a major portion of their time at a center.
13.   People share a common history, beliefs, and values.

☐ Nature and Significance of This Book's Contribution

Since Peterson (1978) first defined the field of educational gerontology as a legitimate field of inquiry, education for older adults has grown haphazardly, suffering from the lack of an integrative theory of lifelong education and from the general view that education in retirement is a luxury for the elite few and not an investment in a human resource. Older-adult education has rarely been considered a serious enterprise either within the field of adult education or the world of higher education. With respect to social policy, older adult education is quite independent of the aging enterprise, which remains predicated, to a large extent, on a model of decline and disability. Education has never been seriously considered by gerontologists as a means for solving the problems of seniors who are less advantaged. This book challenges that dominant view by documenting the potential of the vast majority of retired people, who are healthy and able and neither elite nor wealthy, to remain productively engaged and to contribute substantively to community life. Anyone who has ever watched someone they love die slowly before their eyes over 5 or 10 or 20 years understands that what people everywhere want and deserve is a chance to live fully and vigorously to the end of life.

How do the growing numbers of people who work with seniors make greater use of the resources inherent in the population of retired people? The obvious solution is to offer them an opportunity to improve their skills through personal development and leadership training programs. Obvious as it is, the needed leadership training is seldom offered because such education is not considered a legitimate enterprise and policy makers seldom commit public funds to it. Convincing people to attend training classes is also a barrier.

Leadership training has a significant impact on emergent leadership, but there are many other factors within organizations that prompt retirees to assume leadership roles. Leadership is a complex phenomenon that can be fully understood only by understanding the organizational culture that informs it and is informed by it. This book explores a specific context, the seniors' community center, that depends on senior leadership for maintenance of its services and in which senior leaders emerge. It gives voice to the real-life experiences of seniors within an organizational context and offers a framework that can be applied to any organization both to more fully understand the factors and conditions that facilitate the emergence of seniors as leaders and to remove the barriers. This information will be of special interest to the growing numbers of professionals and volunteers of all ages who work with seniors' groups and organizations, particularly those working in education, recreation, and social services.

The political agenda is clear. Volunteers, community groups, and non-profit organizations must play a primary role in the delivery of supportive services to the growing population of elderly people who require them. Volunteerism takes on new status in this age of social transformation, and those in the third age, or retirement phase, of life are in a primary position to play a leading role.

This crisis—the two faces of age, (1) the increasing number of older people who are healthy and able and (2) the increasing number of people who require social support services coupled with reductions in universal healthcare and social service—represents an opportunity to restore a natural order. The wisdom and knowledge of older adults can be used to help recreate vital, caring, age-integrated communities. This set of conditions legitimizes retirement education as not just a luxury afforded an elite group but a worthwhile enterprise with far-reaching benefits to society. Most important, these conditions require that people take a closer look at the attitudes and assumptions imbedded within organizations that serve seniors.

This book examines how to transform society by focusing on the transformation of individuals within an organizational context. It leads the way back to the mainstream of life for those who have learned to be old and who must now unlearn a lifetime of conditioning and explore the possibilities for growth and development. It offers a blueprint for a new paradigm of old age in which we celebrate the richness and complexity of life experience, struggles, and triumphs; a paradigm that takes us deeper into the experience of older people, the meaning of life and its values, giving us new eyes with which to see and serve the higher needs of older adults. And it provides new hope for a better, more vital old age.

Chapter 1 provides a picture of a world that is aging with a force described as tsunamic, like a tidal wave that is potentially destructive. The challenge is to channel this powerful source of vital energy for the good of humanity. That requires leadership. Chapter 2 begins with a sweeping overview of leadership research, searching again for insights into the kind of leadership that will serve the world best as we enter a new era in human history.

Leadership in the Third Age: Who's in Charge Now?

As for the best leaders, people do not notice their existence. The next best, people honor and praise. The next, people fear and the next, people hate. When the best leader's work is done, the people say, "we did it ourselves!"

—Lao Tzu, cited in Heider, 1988

This chapter focuses on the needs, desires, and aspirations that motivate retired people to assume leadership roles and provides a theoretical framework, a way of exploring and understanding the influences within the culture of organizations that either facilitate or inhibit the emergence of leaders. An organizational culture perspective is essential to uncover the commonly held, yet often unspoken, deeper assumptions and beliefs that are the strongest forces influencing leader and member behavior. Particular attention will be paid to the need for social influence or power and the way in which power is shared throughout the organization. Assumptions about retirement, the role and abilities of retired persons and the extent to which the deep culture of the organization supports the emergence of seniors as leaders will be of special interest.

☐ What Is Leadership?

> Often by leaders we mean no more than those whom fate, luck, and some-
> times intrigue have placed at the head of a particular [group] without refer-
> ence to the quality of leadership which they exercise or its influence on
> others for good or ill.
>
> —Montgomery, 1961, p. 7

There are as many definitions of leadership as there are people defining it. Leadership, its definition and skills, are specific to each situation and culture. Although history is full of leaders from all walks of life who were very old, developing older people as leaders in retirement is relatively new. Human resource specialists are concerned about making better use of the human resources of an aging population. The issue is how to provide opportunities for personal development and feelings of achievement through community involvement. Consider the following questions:

1. Can leadership skills from earlier life (i.e., skills developed in business, education, recreation) be transferred to retirement organizations?
2. Can people learn to become leaders for the first time in retirement?
3. How can the leadership skills of seniors be put to greater use in serving the needs of their groups and organizations

As a prelude to addressing these questions, this chapter begins with a sweeping overview of the history of research in leadership, followed by a focus on leadership and the culture of organizations, and why an understanding of the culture of organizations is essential for the development of seniors as leaders. Given the limited research specific to the context of retirement, a review of the literature from various perspectives (e.g., education, business, the military, philosophy, psychology) is included to provide the reader with an understanding of the various ways in which leadership has been conceptualized and researched, as well as to uncover any conclusions that might be applicable to retirement organizations.

☐ Overview of the Literature on Leadership

This review includes selected summaries and reviews of social science research (Hunt & Larson, 1977; McCall & Lombardo, 1977; Stogdill, 1974) and, more specifically, on treatments of organizational leadership. Ogawa and Bossert (1989) and Yukl (1988) were selected because they presented comprehensive reviews of the field of organizational leadership; Ott

(1989) and Schein (1985) provided insights into leadership from an organizational culture perspective.

Stogdill's (1974) summary of the research on leadership from 1949 to 1970 offers the following rough classification of definitions according to their particular focus on leadership: (1) leadership as group process, (2) the personality of the leader, (3) the art of inducing compliance, (4) the exercise of influence, (5) leadership as an act or behavior, (6) leadership as a form of persuasion, (7) leadership as an instrument of goal achievement, (8) leadership as an effect of an interaction, (9) leadership as a differentiated role, and (10) the role of leadership in the initiation of structure.

In 1976, an academic conference convened at the University of Illinois to provide interdisciplinary perspectives on the state of the art in leadership research and on the evolution of leadership as a field of inquiry. The proceedings, *Leadership: The Cutting Edge* (Hunt & Larson, 1977), were intended to "examine theoretical and empirical directions in leadership believed to be at the cutting edge" (p. vi). The first chapter of the proceedings begins with the perspective of Schriesheim and Kerr (1977): "In common with most other topic areas within the social sciences, the state-of-the-art in the field of leadership is not encouraging" (p. 9). Although the title is provocative, one is left with a sense that if empirical research is at the cutting edge, the cutting edge is not the place to gain a better understanding of effective leadership or practical information on how to develop it.

Hunt and Larson (1977) highlighted three theories of leadership that have stimulated the greatest interest: Weber's (1947) concept of "charismatic" leadership, Fiedler's (1971) contingency theory of leadership, and House's (1973) path–goal theory. The charismatic leader is described as having three dominant characteristics—a high degree of self-confidence, a need for dominance (i.e., power or influence), and a strong moral conviction in what he or she is doing. Charismatic theory has suffered from an absence of empirical research, a problem that House (1977) hoped to remedy by challenging researchers to expand their studies of the leader to include situational variables and effects on followers. Charismatic leadership, as redefined by House (1977), focuses on the qualities of the leader while recognizing the importance of the situation and the effects on followers.

Contingency theory (Fiedler, 1971) holds that leaders are motivated primarily by satisfactions derived from two sources, interpersonal relationships and task–goal completion. This theory is intended to predict the effect of the leader given variability along two dimensions, motivations of the leader (i.e., either social or achievement) and favorableness of the task. The theory is based on a construct that claims to be a measure of the extent to which the leader is relationship motivated or task motivated. The construct is the measure of "least–preferred–coworker" (LPC) and it is a calculation of the regard with which the leader holds his LPC. Clearly, without going any further, there are serious problems with the LPC construct as representing the strength of leader–member relationships that render the theory problematic.

House's (1973) path–goal theory focuses on the influence of the leader and rests on two propositions: (1) the leader's function is supplemental (i.e., it depends on many other things, such as the nature of the task, quality of interpersonal relationships, the structure of the organization) and (2) the motivational impact or influence of the leader depends on the situation. Within any situation, the theory holds, there are two categories of variables to consider: (1) the characteristics of group members and (2) aspects of the environment, such as the nature of the task, the formal organizational structure, and the primary work groups of the subordinates. The assessment of contextual variables is then used to predict the influence of specific leader behaviors on the achievement of group goals. This makes sense but does not seem useful, given a conceivably infinite number of contextual variables within each category (i.e., although the theory is sound, the methodology is a problem).

Schriesheim and Kerr's critique (Hunt & Lawson, 1977) described the extent to which contingency and path–goal theories are flawed and inadequate. From a summary of more than 100 scales, many derived from these two theories, few have been used more than once and 97% reported few validity measures. The authors concluded,

> We seem to test only one or two "dominant" theories . . . that suffer from problems of theoretical inadequacy. . . . Current attempts at measuring and testing hypotheses about leadership phenomena are largely futile. Until new or improved theories of leadership are developed, we shall not be able to integrate whatever findings we obtain. Also, without adequate theory, we shall be unable to construct new, reliable, and valid measures of leadership. Without new measures, we cannot place much faith in any findings we obtain. Thus, with several thousand empirical studies already completed in the field of leadership, perhaps the time has come to place less emphasis on empirical investigation and more on the development of theory to guide research. (p. 45)

Melcher (1977) concluded that over 70 years of study have produced little to increase either our understanding or our ability to predict different effects of different leadership approaches or how to promote more effective leadership. He claimed there is little of value to aid either theoretical or practical understanding.

In summarizing the literature on both leaders and leadership, Ogawa and Bossert (1989) concluded that four basic assumptions have framed much scholarly research:

1. Leadership functions to influence overall organizational performance by affecting members beliefs and behaviors.
2. Leadership is related to organizational roles or offices, typically to the highest roles and offices.
3. Leaders are individuals who possess certain attributes, act in certain ways, or both.
4. Leaders operate within organizational cultures and affect how others interpret events: leaders are cultural shapers and interpreters.

These four assumptions continue to provide the foundation for leadership studies throughout the 1990s with a growing appreciation for the organizational cultural perspective.

☐ What Do We Really Know About Leadership?

Leadership has fascinated philosophers and social scientists since Plato—and probably long before. More than 10,000 books and articles have been written on the subject. Furthermore, it is part of everyday personal and professional experience throughout life that affects people in various ways. If you were asked to name a great leader, who would it be? Gandhi? Joan of Arc? Winston Churchill? Mother Theresa? John F. Kennedy? In commenting on leadership, Yukl (1988) stated,

> The term connotes images of powerful dynamic persons who command victorious armies, direct corporate empires from atop gleaming skyscrapers or shape the course of nations. Much of our description of history is the story of military, political, religious and social leaders. The exploits of brave and clever leaders are the essence of many legends and myths. The widespread fascination with leadership may be because it is such a mysterious process as well as one that touches everyone's lives. (p. 1)

What about your father? Or your mother? Or a favorite teacher who gave you confidence in your abilities and inspired you to be the best you can be? People tend not to think of those whom they know personally as great leaders, even though their influence may have been profound, transformative, or both.

☐ What Makes a Great Leader Great?

I have nothing to offer but blood, toil, sweat, and tears.
—Winston Churchill

Approaches to understanding leadership have tended to focus on one or any combination of the following aspects:

- Qualities and traits of an effective leader
- Skills associated with being a leader
- Different styles of leadership
- Situation or context variables

The traditional approach to understanding the leader has been to identify the qualities and the skills of an effective leader—what is commonly known as the "great man" theory of leadership. From an exhaustive analysis of 163 trait studies from 1949 to 1970, Stogdill (1974) derived the following description of a successful leader:

> The leader is characterized by a strong desire for responsibility and task completion, vigor and persistence in pursuit of goals, venturesomeness and originality in problem-solving, drive to exercise initiative in social situations, self-confidence and sense of personal identity, willingness to accept consequences of decision and action, readiness to absorb interpersonal stress, willingness to tolerate frustration and delay, ability to influence other person's behavior and capacity to structure social interaction systems to the purpose at hand. (p. 175)

It is an exhausting image to maintain during retirement, but that is the image that tends to prevail, the ideal people seek and strive to meet. One might question the sanity of anyone at any age who would freely choose to "absorb interpersonal stress" and "tolerate frustration" when they could be golfing in Palm Springs or cruising in the South Pacific.

☐ Leadership Styles

Different styles of leadership are associated with different situations: some work in some situations and not in others. The laissez-faire style, in which anything goes, often reflects a lack of leadership skill. If someone says, "I guess my leadership style is pretty laissez-faire," it probably means they know little about leadership. About the only time a laissez-faire style works is on an extended vacation. The democratic or participatory style, in which the majority rules, is characteristic of parliamentary or political leadership. It works for some groups but not for others, and only for some of the time. And it means that 49% of the people at any given time might not have their needs met. Shared leadership means people do not simply participate in decision making; the responsibility for leadership is shared among the members. This style of leadership is typical of self-help and mutual aid groups and nonprofit organizations, where the responsibility for leadership is shared among members. Servant leadership is an approach that focuses on serving the individual needs of members.

The leader does not use the group to promote personal goals or organizational goals but listens carefully to what group members want and need and acts accordingly. In retirement organizations, a combination of shared and servant leadership works, for reasons that will become clear later in the book.

Despite his thorough analysis of the research and his elaborate definition, Stogdill (1974) was forced to conclude that "four decades of research on leadership have produced a bewildering mass of findings. . . . The endless accumulation of empirical data has not produced an integrated understanding of leadership" (p. vii).

Subsequently, a group of distinguished social scientists held a conference in New York to consolidate the existing knowledge of leadership. The title of the publication from that conference, *Leadership, Where Else Do We Go?* (McCall & Lombardo, 1978), reflects the sense of futility among empirical researchers at that time. The delegates concluded that they really did not know anything for certain, and maybe all they had succeeded in doing was making a fascinating subject dull and boring. They decided, however, that they had learned much about what to avoid and how to proceed. They felt they may have thrown the baby out with the bathwater in reducing leadership to its common terms and emphasized the need to get at a deeper meaning of the term *leadership* and to explore the motivation of leaders. In particular, the idea of "[H]ow leaders share themselves and through their sharing breathe power and purpose into others" was suggested as an intriguing area for research (McCall & Lombardo, 1978, p. 101). What about motivation to become a leader? Is there an assumption that money is the motivator? That leaders are born? And once a leader . . .

Although considerable disenchantment with empirical research is reflected so far, studies up to this point have been more about *leaders* than about *leadership*. During the 1980s, there was a resurgence of interest in leadership, but with a greater appreciation for context. In his critical review, Yukl (1988) claims some progress has been made in our understanding of leadership. He said, for example, that we know the following:

- There are many different valid definitions of leadership.
- There are a vast number of qualities and traits that can be identified with an effective leader.
- Leadership, its definition, and its essential qualities and skills are specific to each situation and context.

Definitions of leadership have, as a common denominator, the assumption that it is a group phenomenon involving interaction between two or more people. Furthermore, most definitions reflect an underlying assumption that it involves influence exerted by the leader over others. All definitions have in common differences in the specifics of *who* exerts the influence, *why* (for what purpose), and *how* (in what manner). The leader, by virtue of the authority of a formal role, acts to influence commitment to and achievement of group goals. Although these conclusions are not very definitive, they shift the emphasis from theories of the great man to an appreciation for the unique situation and organizational context.

Rather than reduce it to its common elements, leadership ought to be studied with an appreciation for its complexity and a greater tolerance for ambiguity and uncertainty. To learn about leadership in organizations, we turn to organizational theory, a body of knowledge concerned with describing and explicating the structure and function of organizations.

☐ Leadership and Organizational Theory

To understand how leadership functions within an organizational context, one must study the culture of the organization in much the same way that anthropologists study societies and peoples. The organization is viewed as a minisociety that mirrors aspects of the broader culture: the organizational culture shapes leadership. Leadership and organizational culture are two sides of a coin, and one aspect cannot be understood without understanding the other. Whereas the structure of the organization is visible, its culture is implicit, complex, and often difficult to understand.

Culture refers to aspects such as commonly observed behaviors, group norms that evolve over time, dominant values, and the philosophy that guides formal policy. The essence of culture operates at the deeper level and refers to basic assumptions and beliefs shared among members that often operate unconsciously. This deep culture evolves through a history of shared experiences. The organizational structure (i.e., the formal roles and system of relationships among people) indicates how the organization functions. The visible manifestation (level 1), however, must be tested against the expressed views and values (level 2). To fully understand the influences on emergent leadership, one must probe beneath articulated goals and values for underlying beliefs and assumptions (level 3) that are fundamental to the organizational culture. It is at this level where evidence of widely held ageist attitudes can be discovered. The three levels of organizational culture are detailed here:

Level 1: Artifacts (visible, but often not decipherable)

- Art

- Technology
- Visible patterns

Level 2: Beliefs and values (some level of awareness)

- Testable in physical environment
- Testable by social consensus

Level 3: Basic assumptions (invisible, tacit, preconscious)

- About seniors' needs and abilities
- About the nature of retirement
- About the nature of power
- About the nature of leadership

Leadership theory (theories about the qualities, skills, and styles of leaders) and organizational theory (theories concerned with the structure and function of organizations) have generally developed independently of each other. Organizational variables (e.g., task complexity, delegation, reward systems); affect the behavior of both groups and leaders. According to Tannenbaum (1961), "Leaders do not function in isolation; . . . they must deal with followers within a physical, social, and cultural setting" (p. 23).

Recognizing that the scholarly focus on specific aspects (e.g., the qualities or skills of the leaders) within the context of an organization has provided few insightful conclusions, Ogawa and Bossert (1989) offered

> a view of organizational leadership that does not treat it as the province of a few people in certain parts of organizations. Rather, we treat it as a quality of organizations . . . a systemic characteristic. To find it, we submit, one must not look in one place or another but must step back and map leadership through organizations. (p. 1)

In their view, organizational leadership refers to

> the influences exerted by individuals in high level offices through their traits and their actions on the overall performance of organizations. And, more recently, it has been added that this influence of leaders is wielded in and through organizational cultures. (p. 4)

Before the 1990s, organizational theorists generally failed to recognize the extent to which leadership is much more than just a matter of wielding power from a position of authority (Bolman & Deal, 1991; Ogawa & Bossert, 1989). Leadership is something that flows throughout an organization and is not unidirectional, although it is typically hierarchical. Whereas a leadership role (e.g., president, director, chair) typically involves certain tasks, the essence of leadership is the influence leaders have and the qualities they possess over and above the basic skills required to carry out their formal role. Leadership traits or qualities are personal resources on which leaders rely. Because leadership is based primarily on personal resources, more than the authority of office, everyone in the organization can exert leadership. Administrators, directors, or coordinators can fulfill their responsibilities without exercising qualities of leadership and, conversely, as a member of a group, one can inspire one's colleagues or compatriots to undertake new challenges and initiatives. For example, the volunteer in the kitchen who serves the coffee sets a tone among his or her coworkers in ways not defined by an official role and influences the climate of the organization.

Leadership is a relationship between people that Bolman and Deal (1991) describe as "a subtle process of mutual influence that fuses thought, feeling and action to produce collective effort in the service of the purposes and values of both leader and the led." (p. 410).

Furthermore, according to Ogawa and Bossert (1989) organizations are "systems of shared meanings and values. Their structures are cultural expressions. The extent to which meanings and values are shared affects the organizations' solidarity, which is linked to cohesion and cooperative collective action." (pp. 14–15). The formal organizational structure is merely one manifestation of the culture, whereas the organizational culture is the essence of leadership.

☐ Leadership Styles and Assumptions About Human Nature

Although the organizational culture perspective is relatively new, McGregor (1960) explained four decades ago how leadership styles reflect underlying attitudes and assumptions about people. His concept of "theory X" (consistent with an organizational effectiveness approach) and "theory Y" (a more optimistic view of human nature suggestive of the human resources perspective) illustrates how leadership styles or approaches based on assumptions about human nature set up expectations that influence individual and group behavior. Theory X reflects the traditional view of authoritarian leadership, and the rationale for direction and control is as follows: The average human has an inherent dislike of work and will avoid it, and so must be coerced to work. Furthermore, he or she prefers to be directed and to avoid responsibility, has little ambition, and wants, above all, to be secure. This unsatisfied need for security is met by an authoritarian style of leadership.

If, however, individuals have satisfied lower level needs and have an emerging need for achievement and personal development, they may be more willing to become involved in leadership opportunities that are challenging and make full use of their talents. People deprived of the opportunity to satisfy personally important needs typically react by rejecting responsibility, resisting change, and following an authoritarian leader. Members of an organization will continue to follow a controlling leader and will refuse to become more involved and take on responsibilities unless they perceive it as an opportunity to satisfy their unmet personal needs.

Theory Y is based on a more optimistic view of human nature and represents an integration of individual and organizational goals (i.e., the human resources approach). Some underlying assumptions (McGregor, 1960, pp. 47–48) are as follows:

1. Work may be a source of satisfaction.
2. Under proper conditions, humans learn and seek responsibility.
3. External control is not the means to achieve organizational objectives. People will exercise self-direction in service of objectives to which they are committed.
4. Commitment to the achievement of organizational goals comes from the opportunity it presents to satisfy higher needs.
5. The capacity to exercise a relatively high degree of imagination and creativity to solve organizational problems is widely distributed in the population.
6. Under many conditions, the potential of average humans is only partially realized.

The central principle of theory Y is that members can typically achieve their own goals best by directing their efforts toward the success of the organization. Conversely, organizations will achieve their goals best if significant adjustments are made according to the needs and goals of the members. The task, therefore, is to create the best conditions so members feel they can meet their own needs best by directing their efforts toward the success of the enterprise.

The primary goal, according to human resources theory, is to develop an individual's potential. Therefore, to create an environment in which effective leadership emerges, the formal leader creates conditions for personal growth and opportunities for members to meet their needs by taking on more responsible, leadership roles. Management controls people by pushing them in the right direction; leadership motivates them by satisfying their need for achievement, recognition, personal development, and self-actualization. When organizational leadership functions to facilitate emergent leadership, the organization becomes a renewable, sustainable culture of leadership. There is growing recognition that the key to organizational success lies in leadership that functions to realize the potential of every individual member or constituent. Based on 40 years of experience in nonprofit organizations, De Pree (1997) claims that the most effective leaders see potential not merely as self-fulfillment but as expressing stewardship and servanthood. He suggests that the driving force in both profit and nonprofit organizations ought not to be goal achievement, but rather organizations and people that move relentlessly toward realizing their potential. Nowhere is this more critical than in the field of aging in the development of committed, productive, self-actualizing senior leaders in vital retirement organizations. Yet rarely is the link made to leadership in retirement organizations.

☐ The Context of Leadership in the Third Age

I may well die, but I have no plans to retire.

—Margaret Mead

Prompted by colleagues and acquaintances who continued to remain actively engaged in leadership roles well into retirement. Benyamin Chetkow-Yanoov spent many years researching senior volunteer leaders in Israel. He was curious about what enabled such people to continue being active and to "avoid the status of irrelevant old folks." In an attempt to distinguish older individuals who function as leaders from others who do not, Chetkow-Yanoov (1986) analyzed data from 706 questionnaires mailed to retired professionals representing the creative, helping, and service professions. What he found suggests that a pool of talented, third-age leaders who are willing to devote themselves to issues of aging and their profession does exist.

Chetkow-Yanoov concluded that many professional people have no desire to disengage from society and recommended that leadership-training courses be offered by employers as a part of preretirement programming and by colleges and universities as a part of adult education. He further asserted that the continuing competence of older leaders challenges many societal stereotypes and assumptions on which social policy and services to the aged are based.

These conclusions about third-age leadership in Israeli society support a widely held view in North America that retired professionals tend to remain active and involved after retirement. Academic institutions have sponsored a number of programs that foster the active participation and involvement of senior learners. The University of Boston has developed a gerontology program that draws on the resources of senior students, offering productive roles for retirees. Manheimer and Snodgrass (1993) found that in Asheville, North Carolina, seniors are leaders in the community as a result of participation in the Creative Retirement Program, in which retirees participate in a leadership training program that introduces them to the community and offers them opportunities to contribute their leadership skills and life experience as voluntary community leaders. At Kingsborough Community College in New York, senior students in the "Myturn" program participate in age-integrated classrooms; not only are these seniors altering ageist stereotypes, many become mentors and tutors to younger college students (Ginsberg, 1995). Seniors in the Brookdale Program in Applied Gerontology at Bar-Ilan University serve as researchers in the study of aging (Glanz, 1997).

Programs such as these are changing ageist stereotypes of older people as noncontributing members of society. However, these programs generally serve the needs of people who are educationally advantaged, many of whom have been leaders throughout their lives. What about people who are not comfortable in a college or university setting, people who have never been well served by education and do not think it is relevant to their lives? The emergence of leaders for the first time in retirement and a realization of the potential contribution of that vast and diverse population of nonprofessionals would serve as an even greater challenge to societal stereotypes. What are the desires and potential of most older people today that may lead them to become leaders?

Why Be a Leader in Retirement?

Why would anyone who is retired and has the luxury to engage in self-chosen leisure pursuits agree to take on the responsibilities of a leadership role in a seniors' organization? Maslow (1968) and McClusky (1974) had important things to say about what motivates people to continue to develop their human potential to the end of life. Their work, reflecting the human potential movement of the 1960s, holds new insights for leadership in the 21st century and warrants reinterpretation.

Leadership and Motivation

Exploring why human beings behave as they do has preoccupied social scientists and philosophers in much the same way that leadership has. Three major approaches have dominated the field of psychology since its emergence in the middle of the last century: (1) the experimental approach exemplified by the behaviorists (e.g., Hull, Tolman, McClelland, White, Skinner); (2) the psychoanalytic approach developed by Freud;

and (3) the humanistic tradition associated with Maslow, Rogers, and others.

Behavioral psychologists, using empirical methods in the tradition of natural science research, contributed to early understanding of human behavior. Hull (1943) deduced principles of human behavior from extensive, highly controlled laboratory studies of animals and conceptualized motivation in terms of drive-reduction theory. As Peters (1961) suggested, the use of the term *drives* was a way of translating the concept of *need* into mechanistic terms, representing a marriage between mechanical and purposive explanations for behavior: the suggestion is that a predisposing biological condition activates goal-directed behavior. A physical state of tension in the body compels behavior designed to restore a sense of equilibrium or homeostasis. In this tradition, McClelland's (1955) concept of achievement motivation and White's (1958) notion of competence motivation generated considerable interest among empirical researchers for many years.

A second direction in the scientific study of motivation came from Freud, who developed psychoanalytic theories to explain motivations and processes that could not be observed. For those drives that could not be explained by the drive-reduction theorists, Freud posited the notion of the unconscious (i.e., unconscious desires and wish fulfillment).

Both behavioral and psychoanalytic approaches tend to view human behavior narrowly, as determined either by biological drives and impulses or by impulses that are unconscious, pathological, or both. Although the empirical work of the behaviorists is exemplary in its precision and psychoanalysis has contributed to the humane treatment of psychopathological disturbances, both approaches are limited in their views of human motivation.

Maslow and McClusky Revisited

Maslow believed that human potential had always been underestimated within social science. His theory builds on the notion of basic needs posited by the drive-reduction theorists and extends the concept of physiological needs to include higher order needs, incorporating desires and intentions that distinguish humans from animals. The distinction between humans and animals is largely one of will and intentionality; therefore, the individual must be characterized as striving toward a goal rather than compelled or pushed to relieve a tension.

Maslow conceptualized needs as representing the "essence of human lives," and his exploration of motivation involved viewing the individual as a total human being in a natural social environment. Based on the interpretation of case studies of successful and productive older people whom he termed "self-actualizers," Maslow's theory provides insights and tentative explanations that help people make sense of their lives. Maslow's (1968) approach to motivation has particular application to understanding motivation in the third age and, in particular, the factors that might influence retired people to take on leadership roles. Maslow focused on human purpose and intentionality, seeing human development as a process of self-actualization that is continuous throughout life. And one way of actualizing or realizing one's full potential is through expressions of leadership.

Maslow's theory states that human beings are motivated by a hierarchy of human needs that they strive to satisfy. This hierarchy involves five categories, beginning with the most basic needs:

1. Physical needs are the needs of the body for food, water, shelter, and clothing. Humans, like most other animals, have a strong drive toward self-preservation. Satisfaction of these needs is essential to survival.
2. Security needs are of two types: physical and economic. Physical security means being in a safe place; economic security involves having a reasonable economic level and not having to worry about loss of economic resources because of old age, accident, and so forth.
3. Social need refers to the need to feel a sense of belonging, of being an integral and important part of a group or culture to which one belongs.
4. Ego/recognition needs include such things as status, recognition, prestige, respect, and self-esteem.
5. Self-actualization is the highest need. It refers to the feeling of making progress toward reaching one's full potential, achieving both what one wants and is best suited to do.

This system is hierarchical because needs at lower levels must be satisfied first (e.g., physical needs before ego needs). If needs in one area are not met, it is difficult to move up. For example, if physical safety is threatened, it is hard to feel good about oneself or to develop one's full potential: concerns for safety simply take precedence. Figure 1 represents Maslow's hierarchy of need.

Although Maslow's hierarchy is familiar, it is not well known that he reserved his concept of self-actualization for maturity and later life. "I have removed one source of confusion by confining the concept [of self-actualization] very definitely to older people. By the criteria I used, self-actualization does not occur in young people." (1987, p. xxvi). He went on to explain that before people are motivated by the need to self-actualize, they must first develop an identity and a personal value system and become autonomous. They must experience a love relationship, endure tragedy and failure, and attain sufficient knowledge to open the possibility

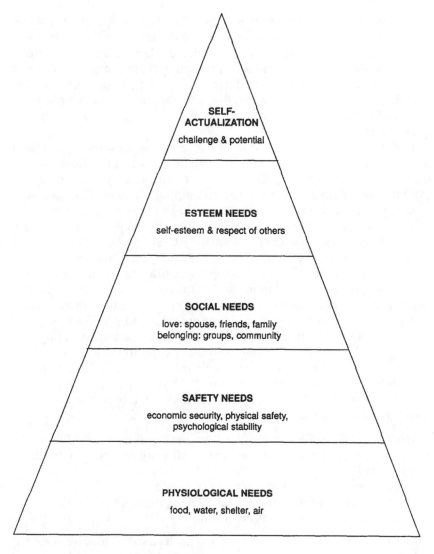

FIGURE 1. Maslow's hierarchy of need.

of wisdom. It is through life experience that the individual becomes a mature, fully functioning human being.

When Maslow's hierarchy is examined more closely, it is clear that the three lower levels or basic needs are met for most older people in third-age societies. The two higher order needs or desires become the focus of interest. To develop their full potential as human beings—that is, to move to a stage or state of self-actualization—people require a foundation of self-esteem and a sense of self-worth. In a culture in which ageist attitudes prevail, few people are able to move to the highest level of development because the needs for status and recognition are largely unmet and therefore particularly strong. If status and recognition are not accorded in the broader society, people tend to affiliate with age-segregated communities to maintain or achieve a sense of self-worth. Figure 2 focuses on Maslow's top two needs: the higher order needs and the desires of people whose basic needs are met.

Maslow's theory of motivation has practical application to organizational leadership and, more specifically, to human resource theory, which has focused on maximizing the fit between individual needs and organizational goals. Human resource theorists support the view that successful leadership emphasizes the needs of people rather than the goals of the organization, and is directed toward satisfying people's need for personal meaning and self-development (Bolman & Deal, 1991).

The third age, according to Laslett's 1987 definition, would seem to be one in which retired people develop their full human potentials. For many, that may involve assuming leadership roles in retirement organizations. The central question is, What kind of social environment makes that possible? Maslow (1987) said that growth toward self-actualization is made possible by a hierarchy of favorable preconditions (i.e., physical, interpersonal, and cultural conditions) that permit individuals to become sufficiently confident to take charge of their own future and become what Maslow called "the fully human person." According to Maslow's theory, some of the preconditions that foster such high levels of personal development are underlying assumptions within organizations:

- Assume in all people the impulse to achieve and do a good job.
- Assume people need to feel needed, useful, successful, and respected (ego need).
- Assume people are trusting and can be trusted.
- Assume the need for connectedness (belonging need).
- Open communication is a prerequisite.

Maslow's theory helps us to understand leadership in later life. It is value explicit, supports an optimistic view of human motivation, and promotes a view of old age as a time for continued personal development. The view that many individuals are continually striving toward the development of their full potential is consistent with Dewey's notion of education as growth and with the concept of learning as continuous throughout life (Cross-Durrant, 1984). Although this seems neither definitive nor surprising, it is important to consider that retirement has never been viewed as a period of continuous personal development for most people. For the rich and powerful, perhaps. For creative artists and

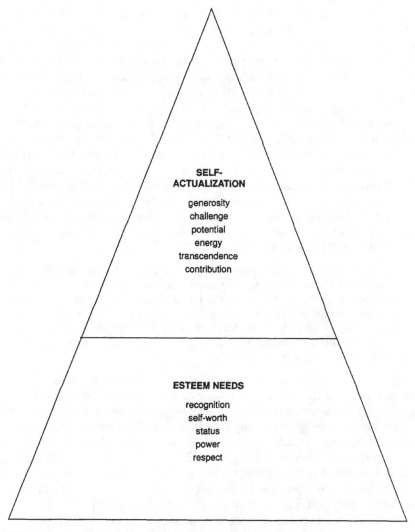

**SELF-
ACTUALIZATION**

generosity
challenge
potential
energy
transcendence
contribution

ESTEEM NEEDS

recognition
self-worth
status
power
respect

FIGURE 2. Maslow's top two—higher level needs and desires.

composers, maybe. But not for the average person. Maslow's theory was based on a small sample of elite and powerful intellectuals, yet the promise of the third age is that self-actualization theory may be applied to most older people.

Like Maslow, American educator Howard McClusky emphasized the development of human potential as a lifelong process. Both Maslow and McClusky defined a need as a condition marked by the lack of something, the existence of which motivates the individual to act so as to achieve a desirable goal. McClusky (1974) identified five needs common in later life: coping, expressive, contributive, influence, and transcendence. The coping needs are most directly related to loss of power experienced as a result of loss of income, employment, energy, and physical health, in which case, financial, health, and counseling education may be remedial. Expressive needs are variously met through recreational pursuits, such as involvement in healthy physical activity, dancing, music, and art.

The contributive need, reflecting the need to feel useful and to contribute to the community, is the one that McClusky claimed deserves greater recognition, because this is the need, he suggested, that must be addressed in making better use of the resources of retired people. The influence need also has particular relevance to leadership. Because of diminishing income, resilience, and self-confidence, power in the social realm is a problem. Older people occupy fewer social positions of real power and therefore have a greater need to become agents of social change. McClusky (1974) further stated,

> Older people have a vital need for [opportunities] that will enable them to exert influence in protecting and improving their own situation, and in contributing to the well-being of the larger society. . . . The result of such programs would be the development of new influence roles and a social climate more favorable for the development of self-respect. Such a program would also shift the emphasis . . . from "doing for" older people to helping them "do for themselves." (p. 336)

The final need is for transcendence, which McClusky defined as the need to engage in activity beyond personal interest, characterized by selflessness and generosity. McClusky identified a need in the later years to transcend the ego and the limitations of the physical body and to develop the secure knowledge that one has achieved some importance beyond this life by contributing to family, culture, and friendship. This is again consistent with Maslow's concept of self-actualization as continuous personal development and represents a variation of the need to make a contribution—that is, to have a driving purpose in life.

McClusky's views are consistent with those of Maslow with particular emphasis on contributive and influence needs. As an advocate of education in later life, McClusky (1974) claimed it is these critical needs and the undeveloped potential of older persons that make education in later life so important. Both McClusky's and Maslow's theories are based on an optimistic view of human beings as striving to develop their full potentials and to contribute to the community until the end of their lives—a view that is becoming increasingly defensible given the growing visibility of active, vital seniors in third-age societies.

A human resources approach applies Maslow's theory of motivation to organizational theory. People may be influenced to become involved, take on responsibilities, and assume leadership roles in community groups and organizations that afford them opportunities to address their needs (e.g., for personal development, power, or influence), while contributing to group or organizational goals. Fundamental to the human resources approach is the role of the organization in meeting the needs of individuals. Consequently, leadership should recognize and address fundamental needs as a way of developing individual potential. What the human resources approach fails to consider is the extent to which approaches to leadership both reflect and derive from fundamental assumptions about people, their needs, and their potentials.

Limitations of a Human Resources Approach

Organizational leadership mirrors dominant forces in society. The human resources approach, which originated in the 1960s, underestimates the strength of underlying assumptions and social forces within the organization as well as the impact of external societal forces on people and organizations (Ott, 1989). In addition, the human resources approach, emphasizing as it does the centrality of addressing individual needs for personal development, requires that individuals recognize and articulate their needs and believe that the organization will address them. It assumes that the director or manager of the organization believes in the untapped potential of every individual. It also requires that individuals believe in themselves and have a keen interest in developing their skills and abilities.

These basic assumptions at the heart of the organizational culture promote internal cohesion and help the organization adapt to external societal forces. Typically, these assumptions are unquestioned within the organizational culture, and they develop over time through a shared history. Understanding and promoting effective leadership in seniors' organizations requires an understanding of the organizational culture. One visible aspect of a culture that promotes leadership is training and education.

Leadership Training

The case has been made for leadership training as a way of influencing people to take on leadership roles in retirement (Chetkov-Yanoov, 1995; Cusack, 1991; Grasso & Haber, 1995; Manhemier & Snodgrass, 1993; Schultz & Galbraith, 1993). The Participation With Confidence project (Cusack, 1991) provides direct evidence that a leadership-training program influences people to take on leadership roles for the first time in retirement. The program's objective was to increase member participation in leadership roles in a seniors' center. A 20-week training program was designed to meet the specific needs and interests of the membership. Workshop topics chosen included assertiveness, time management, communication, confidence building, and tips on healthy aging. Comparison of an activity indicator before and after the program confirmed that participants were indeed taking on more leadership roles.

The evaluation of another leadership-training program provides further evidence of the benefits of leadership training (Cusack & Thompson, 1992). Using the Participation With Confidence program as a foundation, this project involved extensive research and development, culminating in a program model that consisted of 10 workshops reflecting key elements of senior leadership. The program was designed for a wide range of seniors' groups, organizations, and community centers, and those who participated came from various seniors' groups. Most of the participants held formal leadership roles; many were members of the board of executives in their respective community centers.

Despite the positive results from these two pilot projects, what remained unanswered was the extent to which the organizational contexts to which participants returned would either support or thwart their enthusiasm for greater involvement. Do others in their centers believe in and support the development of senior leadership potential? What about the attitudes of others toward seniors as leaders within your organization? Does taking on leadership roles in your organization offer people an opportunity to satisfy needs for recognition, achievement, personal development, influence, and power?

One of the most provocative questions raised in the pilot project was what motivates people to become involved—provocative because it generated lively discussion and debate. When people were asked what motivated them to take on leadership roles, many initially said they wanted to make a contribution and did not need reward or recognition, since recognition and status were not as important as when they were younger. Everyone, with one exception, agreed they needed recognition for volunter work. One participant remained adamant that her motives were purely altruistic. Curiously, 6 months later, she inquired whether her name and contribution would be acknowledged in the training manual (Thompson & Cusack, 1991). Perhaps the kind of recognition people seek is different in retirement. Or perhaps it just differs among individuals. To what extent and in what way does your organization accord the desired status and recognition to its senior leaders?

The question of legitimate power and influence extended to seniors was another issue discussed in the training program. A board member observed that staff from his center met regularly with the governing body for seniors' centers. He thought this indicated that paid professionals had more power and influence and that seniors' were excluded from certain kinds of decision-making processes. He suggested the formal role of a senior leader may be a form of tokenism, extended in a patronizing fashion.

The relationship between professionals and seniors is critical. One leadership trainee felt that staff in her seniors' center "treat us like children." As evidence, she pointed out that when people sign up for bus trips they are asked to register as "seniors" or "adults" and this suggested to her that seniors were not accorded full adult status. When staff were subsequently questioned, they said the label was necessary because adults had to pay full fare and seniors paid a cheaper fare. Nevertheless, the sensitivity to being treated as children reflects underlying issues and attitudes that cannot be lightly dismissed and warrant further exploration. The relationship and specific interactions between leaders or managers and seniors, and in particular the leadership style of professionals, are critical to the empowerment of seniors.

The conception of leadership that professionals working with seniors typically operate from is a variation of the dominant view. Kotter (1990) explained that "leadership involves establishing a direction, aligning people in support of the direction, and motivating and inspiring people to continue moving in the chosen direction" (p. 6). This model, the organizational effectiveness approach, equates the exercise of leadership with whatever is necessary to maximize the achievement of organizational goals. The role of the leader that transcends the particulars of a designated managerial role (i.e., whether that person is called administrator, chair, president, program coordinator, or director) is the responsibility for envisioning a particular group's goal, defining its tasks, and motivating and inspiring other members to achieve these goals. There are a number of general problems with this definition when applying it to retirement organizations.

Challenges With the Organizational Effectiveness Approach

Two major challenges with the organizational effectiveness approach are (1) the authority vested in a single person and potential for misuse of power and (2) the emphasis on organizational goals with little consideration for either (a) the needs, goals, and values of individuals or (b) their life experience, qualifications, and skills.

Apart from the centrality of the particular goals of the organizations, what is missing in the organizational effectiveness model is a code of ethics for respecting the rights and freedoms of individuals. Because organizational goals take precedence and the responsibility for setting and achieving the goals is vested in the leader, whatever methods of coercion and deception the leader uses to motivate and inspire others (be it blackmail, brainwashing, or sexual harassment) may be acceptable. The concentration of power in the leader and consequent authoritarian style of leadership is most often a problem.

The Problem of Authority

The leader who operates from a position of authority and control, even if coercing people for what he or she sincerely believes to be in their own interests, may have an insidiously harmful effect on individual autonomy. Peters (1972) claimed,

> When it is said that a man who brainwashes others, or who settles their lives for them without consulting them shows lack of "respect for persons," the implication is that he does not treat others seriously as agents or as determiners of their own destiny, and that he disregards their feelings and view of the world. . . . He denies them the dignity which is the due of a self-determining agent, who is capable of valuation and choice, and who has a point of view about his own future and interests. (p. 210)

Regardless of whether the leader considers himself or herself to be working in the best interests of those being led, failure to respect their rights and freedoms often diminishes them as persons and may create further dependency on the leader.

In retirement groups, an authoritarian style of leadership is a particular problem for a number of reasons. Because many retired people have lost a certain status associated with the workplace, they may be more vulnerable to loss of confidence and self-esteem if they are not treated with a measure of respect as autonomous persons. Furthermore, many retired people have greater practical experience, wisdom, and knowledge than paid professionals in positions of authority. Collectively, they most certainly do.

Klein (1970), working in the context of seniors' centers in the United States, provided this observation:

> [Older people] feel a lack of respect when they are told what to do, they feel a lack of adequacy when they are not asked, feel put down when things are done for them rather than with them. . . . people are no longer willing

to participate in programs where they do not have rights and are not accepted as equal with people who like to think of themselves as the directors, administrators, policy makers, and leaders. (p. 1)

Seniors need to have a measure of influence and need to be involved in decision-making processes in the groups and organizations to which they belong.

Another problem concerns the ability of the professional to define group goals that address the needs and desires of individual members. The goals of the organization, according to the organizational effectiveness framework, take precedence. Not only does the leader have the responsibility for achieving those goals, the professional is charged with responsibility for identifying the needs and the best interests of members. The needs and goals identified by professionals tend to be consistent with organizational mandates but are not of necessity in the self-defined best interests of individuals. In the case of seniors' organizations, they very often are not. The service-providing organizational model sees the role of the professional leader as providing service to the client. Many people working with seniors interpret this as making decisions for and taking care of older people, goals that are counterproductive to what is really needed in most seniors groups—that is, empowering seniors to take greater responsibility and to share the leadership.

Goals of the Organization Versus the Needs of the People

The dominant view assumes the leader will determine goals that are worthwhile and that others will buy into them to meet their personal needs. In business and industry, everyone's task is to get the job done, and money may well be the motivator. The organizational effectiveness model works in many business contexts simply because money provides sufficient motivation. Such is seldom the case in the third age. The question professionals most frequently ask is one of how can they encourage seniors to become more committed, involved, and willing to share the workload? This suggests a lack of understanding of the needs and values of most retired people, which is essential to their commitment and involvement.

Those working with seniors must consider the nature of retirement and the needs and characteristics of older people if leadership is to serve them well. Within the context of seniors' organizations, mandates are typically broad and unclear (i.e., to serve seniors, to provide recreation). Although organizational goals must take priority, if the mandate is unclear, the professional in charge may interpret it in whatever way he or she prefers. The leader may serve personal needs for power and control while addressing organizational goals to the satisfaction of superiors, yet fail to serve the needs and aspirations of the membership.

Krout (1989) outlined the wide variety of organizational goals reflected in the policy statements of seniors' centers across North America. Some of the broad goals are to serve the recreation needs of older adults, to provide social opportunities, to provide leisure activities, to serve the health and well-being of seniors through recreation and sport, to help seniors feel worthwhile, and to develop self-esteem. Do such mandates reflect the needs, hopes, and expectations of most retired people? They certainly must, to some extent, serve the needs of the 15% of the retired population who choose to become members. What of the more than 80% of the retired population who choose not to become involved? To what extent does your organization serve the real needs, aspirations, and goals common to retired people? What is the real purpose or task of retirement that ought to be reflected in your organizational mandate and public policy?

Third age people want to share in decision-making processes and to be treated as equals with paid staff. A style that combines notions of shared, democratic participation and of servant leadership is particularly appropriate to the context of retirement. The bottom line is, as De Pree suggested (1997), "People are the heart and spirit of all that counts" (p. 13).

☐ The Concept of Shared Servant Leadership

One principle of the human resources perspective fundamental to leadership in voluntary organizations is the notion that people participate in group activities to have their needs met. Therefore, the leader's primary role is to serve the needs of individuals in the group. If we include the needs of each individual to grow, to develop skills and talents, to be recognized, and to experience a measure of power and control, it becomes particularly important to share the responsibilities for leadership among the membership.

The concept of servant leadership is not new, dating back to the writings of the philosopher Lao Tzu (originally addressed to the political ruler of China in the 5th century B.C.). These writings were reinterpreted by Heider (1988) as adaptations for a new age. These prescriptions include, "The wise leader does not impose a personal agenda or value system on the group . . . the leader follows the groups' lead and is open to whatever emerges" (p. 97), and "The group members need the leader for guidance and facilitation. The leader needs people to work with, people to serve.

If both do not recognize the mutual need to [support] and respect one another, each misses the point" (p. 53).

Greenleaf (1977) based his conceptualization of servant leadership on a lifetime of personal experience in various leadership roles, and his theory has influenced many of today's top management thinkers (Spears, 1995). Greenleaf claimed there are two kinds of leaders: the "leader-first" and the "servant-first" leader. Simply put, the leader-first type is the authoritarian leader whose focus is getting the task done, whereas the servant leader is

> sharply different from one who is leader first, perhaps because of the need [for] power or to acquire material possessions. The difference manifests itself in the care taken to make sure that other people's highest priority needs are being served. The best test and difficult to administer is: Do those served grow as persons? Do they while being served, become healthier, wiser, freer, more autonomous, more likely themselves to become servants? (p.13)

Servant leadership is based on a view that the primary role of the leader is to serve the needs of others and reflects an optimistic view of the potential of each individual to become a leader and, in turn, serve others. However, Martin's (1990) study of the social environment of three seniors' centers suggests that many professionals in managerial roles hold deep-seated negative attitudes toward older people as dependent and less able to make decisions or contribute to community life, attitudes that act as self-fulfilling prophecies. The common view that people have less to contribute as they age becomes the framework within which they operate. It is important to consider to what extent your organizational culture reflects both (1) a view of retirement as a time for continuous growth and personal development, and (2) a belief in the abilities of retired people and their potential contribution to leadership.

Chapter 3 integrates foundational knowledge of leadership, organizations, and culture with knowledge of leadership in seniors' groups into a coherent conceptual framework for mapping leadership in any seniors' organization that can assist those who want to work toward positive transformation. The challenge is to become an empowering leader who can transform an organization into a healthy, dynamic, self-sustaining community of leaders. But first, a deep understanding of the organizational culture is needed.

3

CHAPTER

Prelude to Organizational Change

Investigations of the "great buzzing confusion" of life require conceptualizations, that is, views of what to look for, how to look for them, and what kinds of structures, processes and relationships are involved.

—Tyler, 1960, p. 7

The challenge for many who work to empower seniors in groups and organizations around the world is to change the structure of power from a traditional hierarchical model to one that is more inclusive, one that gives all seniors a voice and a greater role to play in decision-making processes. Before one can transform leadership, however, there must be a deep understanding of the culture—the deeper values and commonly held assumptions—that has such a profound effect on organizational leadership.

The purpose of this chapter is to outline a conceptual framework to focus and guide the exploration of organizational leadership. It begins with a perspective on organizations, leadership, and culture based on the overview of leadership in Chapter 2. After the conceptual framework is outlined, a description is provided of how the framework was used to guide ethnographic studies of the culture of the two seniors' centers portrayed in Chapters 4 and 5. The primary purpose of these studies was to uncover the beliefs and assumptions people seldom talk about that have such a strong influence on the emergence of seniors as leaders.

☐ Mapping the Structure of an Organization

An empirical study of a complex organization such as a seniors' center requires a framework, a map that outlines the organizational structure and the roles and relationships of leaders and members. A basic conceptual framework is required that will apply to every organization around the world that serves the needs and interests of retired people, whether the organization is one in which seniors attend university or college classes (e.g., Ginsberg, 1995; Glanz, 1997; Kornfeld, 1997; Manheimer & Snodgrass, 1993; Veelken, 1997), participate in activities and programs at a seniors' center (Grasso & Haber, 1995; Cusack, 1991); or deliver self-help or self-care services (Cusack, 1997; Petty & Cusack, 1989; Toseland, 1990). The task is to design a framework that reflects what the various retirement organizations have in common.

Organizations are dynamic, interactive systems of people with a common purpose operating within a formal structure of roles and responsibilities. They vary in many ways, such as size, structure, history, philosophy, physical environment, and formal roles of responsibility. Organizational leadership refers to a process of influence that flows throughout an organization, and it depends on organizational variables in addition to the personal resources, skills, expectations, attitudes, and beliefs of those involved. The structure of the organization is one visible manifestation of leadership, systems of shared meaning and value add another dimension to the understanding of organizational leadership. Typically, the structure of organizations is outlined in policy guides as a hierarchical flowchart, showing who is in charge of whom. Figure 1 is the typical way of representing organizational structure.

Leadership is the pattern of influence that flows throughout organizations. Those in formal leadership roles (e.g., coordinators or directors) possess certain attributes and act in certain ways, but because influence flows throughout an organization and is not unidirectional, all persons can exert influence. Organizational culture has a strong influence on the behavior of members. Leadership both is *created* by culture and *creates* organizational culture; that is, their relationship is one of reciprocal influence. One can never fully understand the dynamics of leadership without understanding culture. Culture must therefore be incorporated into the conceptual framework of organizational leadership.

☐ Incorporating Culture Into the Framework

According to the organizational culture perspective, culture exists in organizations as it does in society: it is socially constructed, evolves over time,

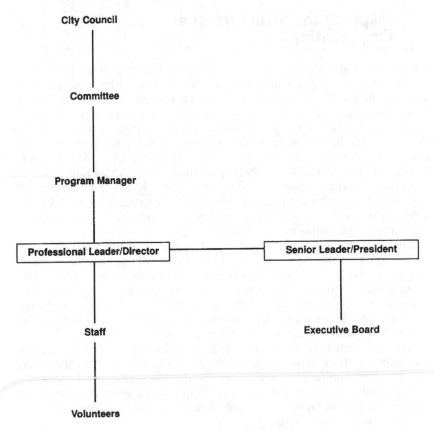

FIGURE 1.   The typical way of representing organizational structure.

and is largely implicit. Culture exists on three levels: (1) visible manifestations (physical environment, rules, policy); (2) shared values, philosophy, views (easily expressed); and (3) underlying beliefs and assumptions. The deeper level of assumptions, which are seldom expressed, is the essence of culture that may provide group energy for action or function as a control mechanism (Ott, 1989). Culture exists between people and is shared by them, so members of a culture understand, although never fully, others within that culture. To understand culture, the focus must be on intersubjective negotiation of the meaning of observable behaviors. The exploration of a given organizational culture involves illumination of the three levels of culture.

Shared beliefs and assumptions that are taken for granted exert a powerful influence over behavior. If, for example, seniors perceive that their leadership skills and abilities are not valued, they will be reluctant to assume leadership roles even when their help is actively solicited. If the common view is that retirement is a time to relax and to be served by professionals, seniors will not be willing to become involved and to assume responsibilities, and they probably will not enroll in a leadership-training course. If, on the contrary, a genuine belief in the skills and abilities of older people pervades the organization, seniors may be more willing to contribute knowledge and assume some of the workload.

The conceptual framework is designed to help the reader identify and understand the influences on emergent leadership by exploring the organizational culture. Consistent with the notion of emergent senior leadership as referring to either a senior assuming the formal role of leader for the first time or a senior leader becoming more effective or moving to a higher level of responsibility, the forces on the senior leader are considered similar to those operating on all senior members.

☐ The Context of Retirement Organizations

This framework—incorporating concepts of organizations, leadership, and culture derived from the literature and professional experience—was originally developed in the context of seniors' centers. It provides a basis from which to explore and define the culture as experienced by its members, and yet is open to new evidence and alternative views, concepts, definitions, and styles of leadership. Initially used to explore the culture of the centers depicted in Chapter 4 and 5, the framework has been subsequently applied to other organizations and proved to be a vital tool in understanding leadership in any nonprofit seniors' organizations in which paid staff and senior volunteers work together to provide service to seniors.

The Role of Theory

The role of theory with respect to empirical investigation is to provide a rough approximation of what one expects to find. Theory has been defined as a general set of ideas through which we make sense of the world (Eisner, 1979; Kaplan, 1964). Theory derived from the literature regarding how leadership functions in retirement organizations, summarized in Chapter 2, serves as clues or as sensitizing agents but not as preconceived ideas that one is testing. In particular, theory should not serve as self-fulfilling prophecy.

Malinowski (1950) made the critical distinction between preconceived ideas and foreshadowed problems. Training in theory and acquaintance with the latest results are not identical with being burdened with preconceived ideas. Grounding in theory arms the researcher with "foreshadowed problems": the more theory he or she brings, the more theory can be recrafted to reflect observations and to see observations in relation to theory. Malinowski (1950) stated, "Preconceived ideas are pernicious in any scientific work, but foreshadowed problems are the main endowment of a scientific thinker, and these problems are first revealed to the observer by his theoretical studies" (p. 9).

A conceptual framework is a construction of analytical understandings and empirical presuppositions. This translation of theory into a network of relationships serves rather like a map; the investigator then begins to explore the context and to gather empirical evidence to corroborate that structure (Eisner, 1979). The results serve as evidence in the confirmation, disconfirmation, extention, and reconstruction of theory. Critical to such an exploratory study is an attitude of openness to the discovery of new insights and possibilities.

When the purpose is to gain a deeper understanding of leadership and the influences on emergent senior leadership in seniors' centers, the center becomes the cultural unit of focus. The conceptual framework is derived from leadership and organizational theory, motivation and human resources theory, organizational culture theory, and preliminary studies in the context of seniors' community centers. A summary of leadership and motivation theory suggests a number of internal influences. A summary of leadership and organizational theory helps to identify three sociocultural categories of influence: organizational variables, relationship variables (especially those between seniors and professionals), and shared meanings and values. These three categories of influence are represented in Schein's (1985) three levels of culture as depicted in Chapter 2. To understand the deeper level of shared assumptions, one begins by exploring the more visible organizational variables and the shared beliefs and values that are more readily expressed in social discourse and observed in the interactions and relationships between people.

Exploring the Culture

The first level of culture refers to the more visible aspects of the organization, including such variables as (1) the history of the organization; (2) features such as policy, programs, special events, ceremonies, and rituals; and (3) the physical environment. The second level refers to goals and beliefs that are readily articulated and reflected in the interactions and

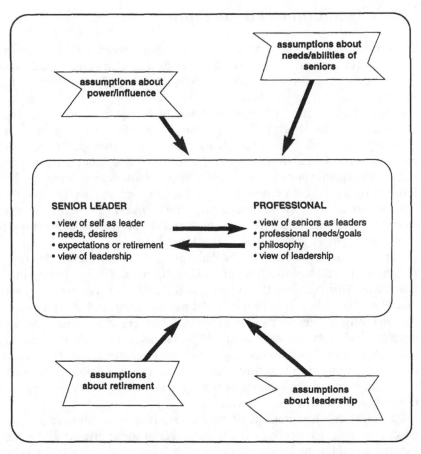

FIGURE 2.   A conceptual framework for exploring the culture of leadership in senior's organizations.

relationships between seniors and professionals: the focus of observations is on social discourse. Variables of interest include the style of leadership, the dynamics of power (i.e., who is in charge), and the quality of the relationship. The goal is to uncover, through probing, interpretation, and negotiation with participants, the third and deepest level of culture. Preliminary investigations supported in the literature suggest that emergent senior leadership may be influenced by assumptions about the nature of retirement, the needs and abilities of retired people, power, and leadership. Figure 2 outlines a conceptual framework for exploring the culture of leadership in retirement organizations. Exploring the culture of organizations draws on a rich tradition of research in ethnography, a method and a process of uncovering the meaning of collective behavior.

☐   A Tradition of Ethnography

The process of understanding the meaning of organizational life is similar to the process an anthropologist uses to study a foreign culture. Although it may be less arduous to achieve an understanding of any culture when a common language and beliefs are shared among the researcher and informants, the culture of retirement may be foreign to those of another age who, without sharing the experience, bring their own values, perspectives, and presuppositions. In its true sense, ethnography requires total immersion in a single culture for an extended time. Studying the culture of organizations is not, therefore, conventional ethnography, but it draws on approaches developed by ethnographers and so is considered to be within a tradition of ethnography. The focus on culture and probing to uncover the pattern of relationships and deeper layers of meaning is what characterizes this approach as ethnographic

Ethnography involves a cultural description that, when applied to organizations, illuminates the fundamental meaning and value of organizational life. This requires that empirical researchers reverse the priority placed on building generalizations and pay attention to particular cases. Ethnography is a descriptive endeavor in which the research attempts to describe and interpret the nature of social discourse among a specific group of people. Both meaning and behavior are described. To produce rich descriptions of the culture, the researcher must be able to both observe the behavior in its natural setting and to elicit the meaning that informs and textures the behavior.

To qualify as ethnographic, however, a study must be more than a rich description. It must probe beneath the layers of social discourse to establish the meaning of visible behaviors, patterns, and artifacts. In other words, its purpose is to *understand the organizational culture.* Ethnography involves socially constructing the meaning of organizational life as it is lived and interpreted by members. This is achieved by carefully observing and recording social discourse and using particular procedures to uncover meaning, shared beliefs, and assumptions. The focus is on intersubjective understanding and negotiation.

Research Methods

Ethnographic methods include document analysis, participant observations, and semistructured interviews. The method that gives a study the quality of ethnography is the iterative interview. In an ethnographic study, interviews are considered joint cooperative enterprises in which the integrity of the participants' experiences is carefully maintained. To uncover cultural assumptions, Schein (1985) recommended the "iterative interview"—a series of encounters between the investigator and various key informants who are members of the culture. He outlined the following steps for uncovering the deeper layers of meaning that define organizational culture:

1. Enter and focus on surprises (record unexplained behaviors).
2. Systematically observe behavior.
3. Identify key informants.
4. Discuss puzzles or hunches.
5. Jointly explore with key informants to find an explanation.
6. Formulate hypotheses.
7. Check the fit of hypotheses with theory.
8. Push to level of assumption.
9. Refine the conceptual framework (or model).
10. Write a formal description (checking fit between theory and discourse view).

Clarifying the layers of meaning in a given culture is a joint effort between the researcher and members of that culture: "The nature of this work can be likened to trying to bring to the surface something that is hidden but not concealed deliberately" (Schein, 1985, p. 113).

How does one draw valid conclusions given such a dynamic and interactive methodology? A contradiction or tension exists between the investigator's need for objectivity and the essential subjectivity and intersubjectivity of culture. Although objectivity can never be fully achieved, it is a goal toward which one must strive. Canons or ways of lending authority and credibility are necessary so that others may judge the validity and usefulness of procedures throughout the research process (Miles & Huberman, 1984).

Validity and Usefulness

With most traditions of inquiry, validity depends on correspondence, coherence, and pragmatism (Kaplan, 1964). Correspondence relates to the fit between the description and the facts. Because values have a significant impact on what is observed in any research setting, self-awareness of the researcher's values is critical, and wherever possible and appropriate, they ought to be articulated. This is essential in ethnographic studies, in which values and presuppositions influence subjective and intersubjective interpretations throughout the investigation.

Correspondence with the facts in an empirical study rests on a form of verification or replicability. Although always difficult, verification is particularly troublesome in ethnographic studies because of the uniqueness of each individual case and the evolutionary aspect of events, conversations, and relationships. To increase the likelihood that an ethnographic study corresponds with the facts, the researcher must check that the structure of events described converges with participants' understandings. This requires the selection of key informants who have a degree of understanding about the focus of the inquiry and the ability to articulate views and concepts. It also necessitates continuous checks on meaning between researcher and informants by direct probing questions in the iterative interviews. Focus group discussions clarify confusions and contradictions. Finally, review of the manuscript by participants is useful to ensure that the text is an authentic representation of the culture as it is experienced by participants.

Coherence refers to the way in which the parts reflect the whole—the simplicity as well as the elegance with which fact and theory, part and whole are integrated and presented. Geertz (1973) emphasized the need to compare the fit of the description of social discourse (i.e., the systems of relations between parties engaged in a communicative activity) with theoretical explanations. In other words, the researcher must verify that the ethnographic text relates to and sheds light on problematic issues identified at the outset. Connections must be maintained between theory, conceptual framework, and the results as text. For example, if the theoretical perspective suggests that assumptions about the power and influence of seniors affect emergent senior leadership, power and influence must be incorporated into the conceptual framework, solicited through empirical data collection procedures, and illustrated through the narrative.

The portraits of how leadership works in two centers are designed to help the reader make sense of his or her own organization. If the reader is to obtain valuable personal insights, the knowledge produced from the research study must be presented in a common idiom so as to be easily understood by all those with whom the researcher is attempting to communicate. Creating a common language is central to ethnographic inquiry and is reflected in both method and goal. Furthermore, when theory is drawn from diverse perspectives and research paradigms, care must be taken to maintain clarity and consistency in the use of key concepts so that the findings can inform people from diverse theoretical perspectives, as well as professionals who are practice oriented. One must consider not just whether the study informs and enlightens scholars, but to what extent it provides insights that inform practical deliberations in other cases and contexts. In this case, it is important to ensure that leaders (paid or volunteer) who are in a position to create change understand the methods and can adapt them to their own organization.

Ethnographic studies describe the particular case in ways that more quantitative empirical studies cannot, the patterns of behavior described may be, to some extent, generalizable. The value of ethnographic research is not in its generalizability, however, but in the rich insights into a particular phenomenon within a given context and its potential to inform practical deliberations in other settings. The narratives in Chapters 4 and 5, may bring to mind similar situations and experiences and prompt reflection on particular styles of leadership and comparisons of relationships within other organizations.

To assist others in exploring and understanding their own organizations in greater depth, a brief description is provided of how research in the tradition of ethnography was carried out and how it produced the narratives in Chapters 4 and 5.

Conducting Research and Writing the Narratives

As a prelude to the study of the culture of leadership in two seniors' centers, questionnaires were mailed to all 55 seniors' centers in a large metropolitan area on the west coast of Canada, to which 20 people responded indicating that they were interested in learning more about leadership. More detailed questionnaires concerning leadership problems and training needs were mailed to this self-selecting sample that had expressed a particular interest in developing seniors as leaders in their centers. The second mailing confirmed that the greatest need was to have more people committed and involved, and many respondents mentioned problems with controlling leaders. All expressed an interest in developing more effective leadership and recognized the need for training.

Studies of leadership-training programs suggested that leadership training would be a key factor in the development of effective leadership (Chetkov-Yanoov, 1995; Cusack, 1991; Cusack & Thompson, 1992; Manheimer & Snodgrass, 1993; Schultz & Galbraith, 1993). Therefore two large urban seniors' centers were selected that were distinguished by leadership training: Carnegie Hall (not the real name) had a history of leadership training, whereas Centennial Center (also a fictitious name) had never offered leadership training but expressed an urgent need for it.

Fieldwork in both centers spanned 12 months, and methods and procedures were replicated in both centers. The study involved the following procedures in both centers:

History: A history of the organizations was obtained through written records and supplemented by information provided by key informants. (One center had a formal written history, whereas the history of the other was obtained from key informants.)

Organizational structure: The organizational structures of the two centers were derived from analyses of policy documents supplemented by discussions with the director and coordinator of the respective centers.

Participant observations: Records were kept of informal visits to the two sites (12 visits to one center over 7 months, 14 visits to the other over 10 months); participation in the annual general meetings; attendance at two monthly executive board and chairpersons' meetings at Carnegie Hall and two monthly advisory board meetings at Centennial Center. All information was recorded that related to the role of senior leaders, skills of leadership, leadership problems at the centers, perceptions of the function of the centers, and factors that motivate seniors to take on leadership roles. The observational record focused on three aspects of social discourse and interactions between seniors and professionals from the perspective of the researcher: style of leadership, dynamics of power (i.e., who is in charge?), and the quality of the relationship.

Interviews with key informants: In addition to professional leaders, key informants were selected in consultation with the director and coordinator of each center. At Carnegie Hall, all seven members of the executive board were interviewed, as well as two others chosen on the basis of their contributions as leaders and their understanding and ability to articulate how leadership functions in their centers. At Centennial Center, the coordinator identified 7 members of the 11-member advisory board and 2 members-at-large.

Semifocused, iterative interviews were conducted by a skilled interviewer provided with a list of questions specific to issues and contradictions arising from the participant observations with respect to the four dimensions of culture. The interviewer was instructed about particular probes and prompts. Interviews lasted about 1 hour and 15 minutes and were conducted in a quiet, comfortable corner of the center. Every attempt was made to simulate an informal conversation, encouraging seniors to speak freely about their views and values. (Nine interviews were conducted in each center.)

Focus group discussions: Interviewees were invited to a final meeting to discuss specific insights and issues raised by the study both for clarification and as a confirmation of the validity of tentative impressions and conclusions.

Final validity check: As a confirmation of the validity of the researcher's understanding of the culture, interviewees read the first draft of the study of their center for accuracy. Table 1 outlines the three levels of culture as they relate to leadership in a seniors' center and the methods used during the fieldwork phase for gathering empirical data with respect to each level of culture.

TABLE 1.   Three levels of the culture of leadership and the corresponding procedures used to gather empirical data

Levels of Culture	Data Collection Methods
Level 1: Artifacts (visible, objective, not always obvious)	
History	Observations
Structural and functional aspects (e.g., policy, roles and responsibilities, programs, events, ceremonies)	Interviews
	Document analysis
Physical environment	
Level 2: Beliefs and values (greater level of awareness than level 1)	
Testable in physical environment	Observations
Testable in social discourse	Interviews
Level 3: Basic assumptions (invisible, tacit, preconscious)	
About retirement	Iterative interviews
About needs and abilities of seniors	Focused group discussions
About power	
About leadership	

☐ Interpreting the Culture of Leadership

Ethnography is both a research style and a written product, a genre that represents culture (Atkinson, 1990). The translation of field notes into results as text representing the culture was a complex process that proceeded in stages. Field notes chronicling interactions and dialogue, the summaries of the history and organizational structure, and transcribed interview data were coded with respect to the four dimensions of culture. Themes emerged through careful reading and rereading. As soon as she was confident that she had an understanding of the dynamics of leadership in the center, the researcher began each ethnography with a summary of the history and organizational structure of the particular center. The narrative of the culture was then constructed by drawing from all data sources.

The narrative account, in which the researcher's voice is silent, first introduces the reader to the physical environment (i.e., level 1 of the culture). The reader is introduced in the manner of a guidebook: the setting is described in concrete terms, features are catalogued, and social types are sketched in. Using the method of ethnographic hypotyposis, graphic passages are used to portray scenes and illustrate themes. Drawing

TABLE 2. Characterization of leadership with respect to the four dimensions of culture

	Retirement	Needs and Abilities of Seniors	Power and Influence	Leadership
Level 1 (visible but not always obvious) History Policy Environment				
Level 2 (values and beliefs) Testable in social discourse Testable in physical environment				
Level 3 (invisible, tacit, preconscious)				

heavily on actual conversations and events, the physical space is peopled with profiles of senior leaders and a professional leader going about their activities in the course of a day, expressing personal beliefs and values (level 2 of the culture), and illuminating influences on the evolution of leaders.

The final stage of the interpretation and construction of the narratives involved a self-conscious interpretation of the culture, a process in which leadership was characterized with respect to the four dimensions of culture. To uncover the deeper level of assumptions—the "meaning of life" in each center—the data were explored with respect to three levels of culture as depicted in the conceptual framework (fig. 2). This process can be visualized as moving through a table of three rows and four columns, with the rows representing cultural levels 1 to 3 and the columns representing the four dimensions of culture. As one reads through the narratives, what they reveal about the beliefs and values that people hold in common—that is, the deep culture—should be carefully considered. The text can be seen, to some extent, as filling in the cells in Table 2.

To determine the influences on the emergence of senior leaders, the focus shifts to individual leaders in Chapter 6. A historical approach is used to illustrate the evolution of leaders and to suggest the influences. Three senior leaders were selected: (1) someone who had been a leader throughout life; (2) someone who initially disengaged during the early postretirement phase only to reemerge as a leader after retirement; and (3) someone who emerged as a leader for the first time in later life.

Personal History and Relationships

The ethnographer must always be aware of the subjectivity of his or her account. Personal history and relations between the researcher and members of the culture influence the account. The researcher's relationship with Carnegie Hall during the course of the investigation was intimate. She felt a part of the culture, having developed a sense of loyalty and commitment to the people and to the center. Furthermore, she saw Carnegie Hall as a model center, exemplifying a style of shared, servant leadership that she had come to believe works best in a community of seniors.

In Centennial Center, her status from the beginning was that of professional consultant and academic researcher. Preliminary visits to the center provided evidence of a traditional approach to leadership common in many other centers that was highly problematic. She saw Centennial Center as emphasizing delivery of recreational programs and services, rather than developing the personal potential of seniors. After the completion of the research, she continued to work with Centennial Center, researching and developing leadership programs. The transformation of leadership within that center has been extraordinary. In many ways, the evolution of leadership in Centennial Center provided the model for creating a culture of leadership in retirement organizations outlined in Part III.

Ethical Issues and Sensitivity

In addition to identifying a style of leadership in one center that was problematic, the researcher constantly wrestled with the fact that she had privileged information about the personal lives of real people that she was exposing for the purpose of education (their own, in particular). She made every attempt to preserve anonymity and was careful to represent what might be considered negative qualities as vulnerabilities and to emphasize individual strengths wherever possible.

As the study proceeded in Centennial Center and the researcher gained a more intimate knowledge of the people, she developed a greater appreciation of individual strengths and greater sensitivity to vulnerabilities. She saw the people at Centennial Center coping with problems created by the hierarchical structure of power and authority in the community (e.g., the smoking bylaw and the parking problem) and by newspaper accounts that misrepresented their center, and she developed great respect for the administrative skills and personal integrity of the coordinator. As well as a greater appreciation for the powerful impact of the surrounding culture in which the center is imbedded. Centennial Center is literally fighting to change the negative stereotypes in the broader community—a very different political and economic climate than that surrounding Carnegie Hall.

The Question of Truth

Ethnographic research is highly selected. Awareness of bias, constant checking with individuals to clarify confusions and contradictions, and participants' reading of the manuscript served to ensure that the portrayals of the centers were valid—that is, true to life. However, as Heraclitus famously observed, "You can't step in the same river twice." Like a photograph, the narratives represent an authentic picture at a particular time and at a particular stage in their evolution—snapshots of two seniors' centers in a moment in time.

PART

II

PORTRAITS OF LEADERS AND LEADERSHIP IN ACTION

Part II contains the real-life stories of leaders and leadership in action within particular contexts. The stories in Chapters 4 and 5 are drawn from rigorous explorations of two retirement organizations using the conceptual framework developed in Part I and ethnographic methods to construct the stories and portraits. Vignettes portray lived experiences and voices tell the stories, stories that reflect the real needs and desires of seniors and the negative attitudes and hidden assumptions that limit the possibilities for purposeful, productive engagement. Chapter 6 focuses on three leaders, illuminating the influences on their development as leaders and the rich, often unexpected, rewards they experienced. Discussion related to common leadership issues and what can be learned that is applicable to leadership in organizations throughout the world is presented.

Carnegie Hall:
Portraits of Power and What
We Can Learn

Vital organizations exude health and energy and enthusiasm. Like vital
people, they are full of hope and anticipation for things to come.

—De Pree, 1997, p. 99

This chapter tells the story of a seniors' center in a city of 40,000 people
on the west coast of Canada. The center was named Carnegie Hall because
it was a place where seniors were given the opportunity to pursue their
passions and encouraged to display their skills and talents. The characterization of the world of Carnegie Hall begins with a history of the organization described in terms of evolving leadership, programs and activities,
and perceptions of seniors. The organizational structure is outlined,
including the external political structure and internal politics expressed
in the mandate and formal leadership roles. The picture painted captures
a moment in time and begins with a physical description of the setting, followed by an account illustrating interactions, relationships, and
patterns of influence. The narrative portrays the meaning of life for
people who work and play in Carnegie Hall—the deeper beliefs and
values commonly held. The chapter concludes with what the narrative

reveals about sharing leadership and empowering seniors that can be applied to other settings.

It's 4:00 p.m. and time for tea and a chat. The bingo players are spilling out. "And all I needed was one lousy *b*, just one lousy *b*—and Ethel beat me to it again. I swear those balls are fixed." Florence is listening attentively to the distraught woman. The president is in the director's office going over details of the chairperson's meeting. Fresh tea and muffins wait in the kitchen, and a pot of coffee is brewing. Strains from "Flight of the Bumble Bee" emanate from a distant piano—a 95-year-old woman practicing for her next lesson.

☐   In the Beginning . . .

On July 23, 1958, Her Royal Highness Princess Margaret was involved in a number of civic events commemorating the 100th anniversary of the founding of British Columbia, and the main event of the day was the inauguration of an entirely new type of recreation center—one designed specifically for seniors.

Despite the reported Royal Proclamation that "Carnegie Hall is a marvelous place," some people were concerned about whether the center would be well patronized or would become a sort of white elephant. Establishing the need for a seniors' center had been difficult. Some members of city council were of the opinion that a center for "old people" was an unnecessary extravagance and would be unpopular. Some thought seniors would not identify with a center for elderly people.

As soon as the council was convinced of the need for a seniors' center, various sites were considered. The one first chosen was a quiet place. One person remarked,

> Some people had actually thought that the location was suitable for "older people" on the grounds that it was near a hospital. Others had taken the view that seniors wanted a quiet place where they would be out of the main stream of life, away from disturbance by children in playgrounds.

Residents who learned of the project objected to the use of land for a seniors' center. The director of recreation objected to the location for other reasons. His view was that, "far from wanting to be tucked quietly away, seniors preferred to be where the action was." To settle the matter, the director attended a conference on the aged at a nearby the university with instructions to consult with experts from around the world. He toured facilities in the United States, and it is reported that "he was surprised to find two or three Cadillacs in the parking lot at Menlo Park, a seniors' center in San Francisco. When he queried this he was told that the well-to-do can be lonely too and need to socialize." (It is commonly assumed that people who have means do not attend seniors' centers.) Plans were finalized for the building, and Carnegie Hall was acclaimed as the first municipally owned seniors' center in Canada.

As a leader in seniors' center programming, Carnegie Hall has been studied by many other municipalities that want to establish similar centers. In the beginning, no age requirement was set. At that time there was no need because it was assumed that no one would want to join a seniors' center who was not old.

☐ Leaders Past and Present

Since 1958, Carnegie Hall has been served by four directors. The first director (1958 to 1975) is described as having the ideal attributes of a leader, and her sympathetic and understanding attitude made her the ideal supervisor of a seniors' center. Although she had no prior experience working with seniors, she learned quickly and was receptive to new ideas. She believed that the best way to operate a seniors' center was to involve members in decision making. She might give advice and suggest programs but implemented only those ideas that reflected the wishes of the membership. One of her greatest attributes was her ability as a conciliator, always able to deal with problems, always smiling, and never rushed.

The current director, Jo-Ann (not her real name), was formally trained and possessed a degree in recreation. She had also been through a 2-year training period that introduced her to the operation of a seniors' center. Jo-Ann has a vision of the center as a one-stop shop for seniors, and she continues to work with staff and seniors to create stronger links with service providers in the community. One of her first projects was to establish a hot lunch program; another priority was the training of a contingent of senior office volunteers. The highly successful peer counseling program, with its office permanently located in the center, exemplifies her vision by providing both outreach to the community and much needed on-site service.

Jo-Ann has worked toward putting seniors in charge of programs and services, with staff in place to assist them in addressing self-defined needs. Both assume primary responsibility for resolving problems and conflicts, and dealing with sensitive issues. Although final responsibility for the operation of the center rests with the director, that responsibility is being shared, to varying degrees, with presidents of the association.

☐ Background and Current Activity

The center is intended to be a pleasant place to visit, have a chat, or meet a friend for lunch, but the focus of operation is on the programs and activities, which initially emulated those provided in seniors' centers in California. In the early days, activity programs were traditionally recreational in nature—crafts, quilting, bingo, bridge, whist, dancing, carpet bowling, billiards, and music. Later the program was expanded to include yoga, walking, hiking, pottery, and painting. Programs offered occasionally included income tax clinics, foot care, wine making, a dining club, senior softball, conversational French, line dancing, a stamp club, stress management, history, genealogy, piano lessons, model airplanes, and theater outings.

Over the years, special committees have been established in response to member needs and interests. A grievance committee was initially established to deal with complaints. In the early days, educational workshops were reported to be a luxury the center could not afford.

The activity committee roster currently has 34 activity groups representing three different types of participation:

Ongoing activities such as bingo, bridge, carpet bowling, dance, painting, quilting, songsters, and crafts

Services such as peer counseling, lectures on health topics, and sick and shut-in outreach

Special events such as theater outings and travel club

In recent years, a series of programs of an educational nature focused on building self-confidence and leadership skills. Members of the board secured funding from the federal government and have benefited from the training. Although educational programs were considered a luxury in the early years, the director, staff, the executive now share a conviction that lifelong learning is critical to healthy aging, and training ensures a supply of committed and able senior leaders. This is key.

In summary, the history suggests a number of themes and trends. Despite an element of controversy within both city council and the community, city officials conferred a certain status and recognition on its elder citizens from the beginning (symbolized by Her Royal Highness' attendance at the inauguration). With a commitment to providing the best possible center for seniors, commissioners consulted outside experts, visited centers abroad, and attended professional conferences. Their message was that seniors were valued members of the community who want to be where the action is and visible in the community.

The present director is giving seniors a greater piece of the action by sharing more of her responsibilities with senior leaders and developing their leadership potential. Evidence of the growing involvement of seniors is reflected in the trend from traditional recreational activities (e.g., bowling, bingo, crafts) toward a greater diversity of programming that includes service-oriented and educational programs, a trend consistent with the evolution of community programs and services for seniors across North America.

The historical account is an overview of styles of leadership. A deeper understanding of how leadership currently functions in Carnegie Hall begins with a description of the formal structure of the organization and the responsibilities of key personnel, as outlined in the center's policy guide.

☐ Organizational Structure

A policy and procedures manual, which is given to all new members, defines the formal structure of power relations and the roles of key people. The mandate is explicitly stated as providing "opportunities that will help satisfy the leisure, social and educational needs of senior adults; and to provide an environment where members feel positive self-worth through acceptance by others, belonging, recognition, contribution, and achievement."

The Carnegie Hall association consists of the membership (approximately 2000 people aged 50 and over) and an elected executive board that includes a president, vice-president, second vice-president, third vice-president, secretary, treasurer, and past president. There are 34 activity groups whose members typically elect a chairperson, a vice-chairperson, secretary, and treasurer to represent them and provide links with the executive and the director. Figure 1 is a flow chart showing the formal organizational structure.

The business of the center is conducted through a schedule of general and special meetings. An annual general meeting is held once a year to hear the annual reports and on alternate years to elect an executive board. A monthly meeting of the executive and chairpersons of each activity is chaired by the president. Its main purpose is to provide a forum from which members can work toward more enjoyable and satisfying activities. Issues not resolved at the annual ageneral meeting are returned to the executive and director for a decision. Special meetings can be called by the president, director, or executive.

Membership Profile

As the population ages, the average age of the membership is increasing, and women outnumber men by a ratio of 3 to 1. This is a culture that is

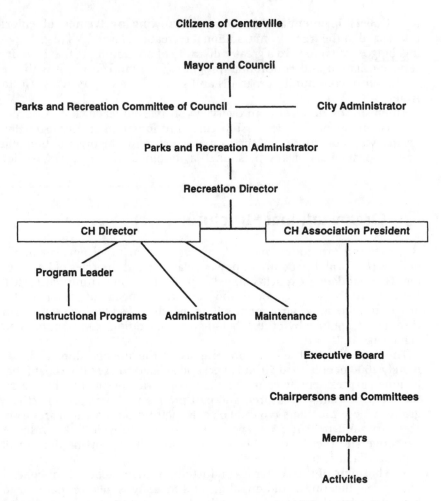

Figure 1. Internal and external organizational structure of power in Carnegie Hall.

predominantly female both in its membership and its leadership. Because few older women have played formal leadership roles in their working lives, many may not see themselves as leaders and require encouragement, support, and training focused on building confidence in their leadership abilities. Without such training, women are often content to let the minority of men take charge; this is not the case at Carnegie Hall. Furthermore, although men are equitably represented in leadership roles, few men take advantage of the training programs.

The account of the history, organizational structure, and profile of members provides a backdrop against which the day-to-day events of the center unfold.

☐ Welcome to Carnegie Hall

The center is a large modern, one-storey brick home set in the center of an expansive park surrounded by an adventure playground, tennis courts, and baseball fields. Three feet away, an old-fashioned two-storey building houses the administrative offices of the parent organization, the Parks and Recreation Department.

It is 8:45 a.m. when a tall, thin, white-haired man with one eye strides up the ramp toward the door. He says of retirement:

> This business of retirement? The way I see it—it's all attitude. You get up in the morning and you have a certain feeling, but you have no idea how the day will go and what will happen. When you get up and go to work it's different. Some days you feel rotten, and just want to stay in bed. But once you get to work you forget about yourself and the day gets better as it goes along. Lots of men just can't wait to retire so they can sleep in. After they've had a chance to sleep in a few times, then what? There's nothing else. A man has to have a hobby. It's just no good if you think too much and get into yourself. You need something to occupy your mind. I have no problem because I love to garden.

It's 8:55 a.m. as the door opens. Marilyn, a vivacious woman of 64, greets all who enter with a cheery hello. A sign says, "Welcome. Your hosts for today are Marilyn and Lawrence." Marilyn first joined the center 6 years ago when she was prematurely "put out to pasture" from her job. She didn't "come here with problems" and doesn't "feel like a senior." When someone told her Carnegie Hall had a good exercise class, "I came down, looked in, and thought, 'Oh God,' because it was full of white heads and they were playing cards and smoking . . . and I thought, 'this isn't for me.' " She came in anyway, and there was "just something about the way she was greeted by staff and members" that convinced her to stay.

Not long after, the director asked her to represent the center at an important civic event. Marilyn has a background in theater. Formerly a singer and dancer, she loves being in the limelight, and the opportunity to take part in that prestigious event was important and rewarding for her. That event, coupled with a leadership training program, gave her the confidence she needed to address a group of people gathered at City Hall: "I don't like my voice, and I have always worried about people being critical. But the more I push myself to speak up at meetings and in front of groups, the easier it becomes and the more I enjoy it."

Just inside the door is a circle of soft rose and turquoise chairs, and it is often said, "What a good choice, you know a committee of members picked them." A sign on the door beyond identifies the senior peer counseling office. Evelyn, a woman in her 70s with severe rheumatoid arthritis, is on the phone with the public health nurse, recording information about a client who is being referred for counseling. As chair of the peer counseling program, Evelyn attends the chairpersons meetings as well as various meetings in the local community, and she sits on two provincial senior peer counseling boards. Her motorized go-cart is ready at the door.

When Evelyn first joined, she lacked confidence and was "barely able to put two sentences together." She had been ill after her husband's death and did not know how she was going to survive on her own. She needed to know what resources were available in the community in case she required assistance. When the peer counseling program began, the director, Jo-Ann, asked if she would be interested in taking the training. Jo-Ann pushed her and people helped her: she felt they had confidence in her. She later reflected,

> The educational programs helped, and my confidence grew as I got more involved. Being involved builds self-esteem, and especially if you get acknowledgment for what you are doing. People are afraid of criticism because they are losing some of their faculties. They'll say, "Oh, I can't see very well" or "I can't hear very well." But they can still use their heads.

Evelyn joined the peer counseling program because it was something she could do, despite severe arthritis. Her background in nursing helped her counsel, although it required learning new skills. "I'm motivated by the learning and it keeps my brain working,. . . keeps me from thinking about myself. I see people worse off than I am and it makes me think how lucky I am." She is reluctant to acknowledge her leadership skills, but says she has always been an organizer with a good memory. She is humbled by the fact that others in the center find her an inspiration.

In a far corner of the front office, Louis, aged 70, pounds the keys of an old electric typewriter. An avid lawn bowler, he joined the center because he wanted "a place to come and play snooker when it rains and I can't go lawn bowling." As secretary of the center, he keeps track of all correspondence and keeps the minutes of the monthly chairpersons meetings. He prepares six or seven pages of typed notes each month, which often requires "two full days of hard work."

Formerly a banker and a business manager for a chain of newspapers, Louis retired early for health reasons. He was helping out in the kitchen at Carnegie Hall one day a few years ago when someone convinced him to run for secretary "because they couldn't find anyone else." He felt well qualified to handle the job of secretary and agreed to take it on.

As a leader, Louis is a hard taskmaster. He says of his leadership style,

> I like things to be done right and I don't want to come to a meeting and find someone didn't do it. I am very organized. As president of the lawn bowling, I don't do a thing, just organize and others do the work. I may tread on a few toes, but if I am given a job, I do it.

On the other hand, he reflects, "I don't like to hurt people's feelings . . . and I don't like to be hurt, either . . . in business or in relationships." (Oddly enough, although Louis doesn't like to have his feelings hurt, he is not afraid to "tread on a few toes.")

Louis, like many men in leadership positions, did not take the leadership-training course and never inquired about his responsibilities. When he learned the ropes, he found it interesting and challenging. Aware that the center was becoming a big business, he identified a number of changes he believed would make the organization run more efficiently. He was, however, unable to implement the changes because, as secretary, his power was limited. Also he has been known to lose his head at executive board meetings. He cannot say he really enjoys his job, although he has a strong sense of loyalty to people and to the center. However, if Louis does not enjoy his job as secretary, one wonders why he is really doing it, when he could be relaxing, playing bridge, and lawn bowling, which he does enjoy.

"May I help you?" A cheerful woman leans over the reception desk to assist a woman in a motorized wheelchair. Like Marilyn, Liz, now aged 71, enjoys people. She also originally came for the exercise classes. When she returned to Carnegie Hall after surgery, a member of the staff asked if she would help out at the reception desk. She describes her experience as follows:

> I got more involved as time went on. Last year I came to help with the elections and they needed a third vice-president. The director said, "Try it, Liz," and I did. I got involved because I just have to have someone to care for and this is a place for me to care for people. The staff are just like my own children, and I love them all.

With 38 years as a salesperson, Liz is used to dealing with people. In describing her skills, she says "I treat people like I like to be treated: I don't talk down to anybody. And somewhere along the way, I think I developed the ability to bring out a sense of humor in people." As a wife and mother who held a prestigious office in a provincial service organization, she had to be a good organizer. Liz is proud that "her family never went without a meal." As third vice-president at Carnegie Hall, she has been able to use both her organizational skills and her people skills as convenor of the annual thrift sale.

Liz has achieved recognition for what she does, and feels a great deal of satisfaction when people say that something she organized went really well. She admits, however, that her self-confidence comes and goes: "It's almost a year since my husband died, and I'm feeling stronger. I still haven't got all my confidence back. Working as a volunteer in the office has helped to build my confidence, and so have the educational programs."

On the couch around the corner from the office, a man in his 80s with tufts of white hair radiating from his head sinks into the chesterfield, adjusting the remote control to a favorite program. Buzz used to spend much time playing bridge, until one of the bridge players asked him to leave because he shook too much and was upsetting everybody else at the table. Buzz left the bridge table, but not before asserting himself: "Someday, when you are as old as I am and you can't stop shaking and you can't hold your cards, I hope somebody will be just as nasty to you as you have been to me." But it did not end there. Buzz returned to the bridge table the following week with a cardholder. (Sensitivity and tolerance are key to effective leadership.)

It's 10 a.m. and time for the executive meeting to begin.

The Executive Board Room

The purpose of the monthly executive meetings is to address issues and concerns, to initiate new directions in the operation of the center, and to prepare for the chairpersons meeting that follows. The group is gathered around a large table as Jo-Ann, the director, arrives saying, "Gee, we all look so efficient—just like a corporate board meeting."

Jo-Ann is a key player in these meetings, as she is in all operations of the center. Her vision for the center includes specific goals, some of which were reached with renovations that were completed last year and the institution of many on-site services. She sees one of her primary roles as an initiator of ideas. She describes her philosophy in this way:

When I want something to happen, I talk about it. I plant some seeds. But I've planted lots of ideas that didn't take hold. It's nice when there is fertile ground. The peer counseling was my idea and I had to sell it because it was new. Timing is everything. I tried to promote intergenerational programs 10 years ago and we weren't ready. Now it's coming back and the initiative is coming from them. It doesn't matter who owns it. It is wonderful to see an idea take shape and grow. My role, and the staff's, is to assist the seniors in doing what needs to be done. It's amazing what seniors have accomplished around here. The sky's the limit. Now the goals I see involve promoting personal growth for members and staff, continous problem solving of issues as they arise, creating new and innovative educational programs, and improving programs and services already in place.

Jo-Ann is sensitive to the needs of the seniors, as evidenced by her remark about her role in "planting seeds" but waiting for seniors to pick up on the ideas and then giving them the credit. According to Heider (1988), when the best leader's task is done, the people will say, "We did it ourselves." And that is exactly what happens in Carnegie Hall.

Jo-Ann thinks it is particularly important for both staff and members to be motivated and challenged. She reflects,

> What makes this kind of work exciting is being involved in something new and unique that people can hang their hats on and get some recognition. Carnegie Hall has always had recognition throughout its history and the challenge is to stay on the leading edge of things. I get the most enjoyment from seeing growth in the seniors and the staff. It's a real pleasure to watch other people blossom.

Margaret is a powerful woman in her 70s whose presence can be felt in every aspect of the operation of the center. She sees the role of president as a full-time job, and she takes it just as seriously. Margaret has always been a leader, managing her father's business when she was 18. She sees Carnegie Hall as a business and fulfills her role with an emphasis on efficiency. Although she admits that a certain amount of status, recognition, influence, and power comes with the job, that is not, she says, why she took it on. Rather, "I took it because no one else would. Perhaps there is an unconscious need. I'm a workaholic and I need something I can put my all into. I traveled extensively before I got involved, and to me that is superficial." Margaret's claim that she took on the job because no one else would leads one to question her motives further. Her admission that she is "a workaholic" who has a need to "put her all into something" is insightful. She uses the language of traditional leadership from the workplace environment. The words she and Louis use when speaking about people in the center are in contrast to the words that other members of the board use.

Like that of many others, Margaret's exit from the workplace was premature and left her feeling unappreciated. As a result, she lost much of her self-confidence. She also missed the friends and connections with stimulating people that her work at the university provided. She knew, however, that she could not "sit around reading *National Geographics* all day," and it was not long before she decided she had to "pull up her socks." She says of her first visit to the center, "The first time I came to Carnegie Hall I thought, this isn't for me because there were old people sitting in the lobby and they had wheelchairs and walkers, and as people get older some of them don't look after themselves as well." She attended a session on financial planning and took out a membership but did not use it for some time. When she returned, she joined the fitness class. She had not come to volunteer; as a single parent raising four daughters, she had always worked and did not know what volunteering was about. But when asked, she thought she would give it a try. Margaret says of her experience as a volunteer, "When I started to work in the office, I knew I had the skills, but I lacked confidence in myself. I had a chance to display my competence when I organized the peer counseling office, and my confidence slowly returned."

Margaret started the first hiking group. When she found she needed another challenge, Jo-Ann came to her with an idea about a new program that would focus on building confidence while developing group leadership skills. Recognizing that many others in the center shared her experience and lacked confidence in their abilities, Margaret did not hesitate to become involved. She says of her motivations, "If I'm asked and it's a challenge, I'll do it. It doesn't matter what the challenge is. If something can be done, and I can make it happen, it gives me confidence. The leadership course helped and my confidence just kept building."

In consultation with the director, Margaret sets the agenda for the executive meetings, allowing considerable flexibility and an opportunity for members to present new ideas and issues. However, she is clearly an authoritarian leader. At this particular meeting, the first item on the agenda is a proposal for a project that emerged from a public speaking course recently offered in the center.

The adult educator who facilitated the course was invited to the meeting, and Margaret outlines a proposal for a project to train seniors as researchers and involve them in leading-edge research in the field of older adult education.

Director: *Part of the research could be to find out what you people want for educational programs. Learning about retirement issues could benefit a lot of people.*

Past President: *We need to look to the future. There is a potential here for all members to benefit.*

Third Vice-President: *This project sounds like an exciting new challenge.*

Secretary: *Who would fund it? Government?*

President: *We're not sure about funds at this stage. Seniors don't generally know a lot about research and we need to be more aware, especially when we have to be responsible for getting our own funding for educational programs.*

Secretary: *What's in it for the people who don't usually get involved?*

Treasurer: *Those of us who have been taking personal development and leadership courses have seen how people progressed. We need to include new people because they have knowledge we don't have. I've seen a change, younger people are retiring and are becoming interested in being involved. There is a different outlook on retirement. We need to address the needs of this new kind of retired person.*

Director: *We also need some direction on where to go from here as far as educational programs in the center. We need more research and information and then we can move forward in directions that will benefit our membership.*

Treasurer: *I'm interested in research for my own learning. Seniors in years to come won't just want activity, they will want a greater depth of knowledge and engagement.*

In contrast to the president's approach, the past president's participation in meetings and activities at the center reflects a much different style of leadership. Fred, aged 68, has always been a person who jumps in with both feet and invariably finds himself in a position where people look to him for guidance. He describes his philosophy as one he learned from his mother: "Honey draws more flies than vinegar." Fred believes that everyone you meet should be considered a potential friend: "You can benefit from their experience and they can benefit from yours." He admits he may not be quite as efficient as he should be but considers some things less important and worthy of Fred's approach to leadership is casual and friendly; his emphasis is on people and making them happy. He says,

> I'm approachable. I take the time to listen to people's problems and complaints, and I offer a few suggestions. Then they feel good. I get satisfaction out of that. Why make people feel bad, when with a little bit of extra effort, you can brighten their life?

An ongoing concern is whether the people who participate in activities are paid-up members. One week during the year, the association addresses this concern by conducting membership checks. The following dialogue shows how the board deals with a sensitive issue. The director plays a key role in keeping the group focused and in being sensitive to others.

Director: *Second Vice, do you want to speak to the subject of membership checks?*

Second Vice-President: *Many of the activity groups are not checking to be sure everyone's membership is paid up. The problem is many of these people are active around the center and they do resent you checking.*

Secretary: *Why do people get so upset when you ask for their card? One guy actually said, "Is this a police state?"*

President: *I want to tell you what I overheard at lunch. This younger person who isn't a member was having lunch with a group of seniors, and she said, "Uncle John is coming for a month and for the price of meals, we'll just bring him here everyday."*

Second Vice-President: *Maybe people don't know you have to be a member to eat here.*

Secretary: *Could we consider posting a notice?*

President: *People don't read signs.*

Director: *In our policy and procedures manual, it says, "Guest passes are available . . . visitors may be a guest for the duration of their visit." That means Uncle John is more than welcome. And out of 200 people we checked, we found only four people who weren't paid-up members. Why not let it go? For the hard feelings we cause, it's not worth it.*

Second Vice-President: *I like that attitude. We need to look at it as they haven't done anything wrong, they just misunderstood.*

Director: *It really is amazing to me how many new people there are.*

President: *Well, when I first came here there were a lot of old people and I didn't stay, because it didn't seem like it was for me.*

Third Vice-President: *One old man I was talking to the other day said, "Why would I want to sit around and play cards and see all those old faces?"*

Second Vice-President: *I guess he doesn't have a mirror.*

A challenge to the leadership skills of executive members is how to contribute to the effective operation of the center while maintaining sensitivity to the needs of members. With the center expanding and becoming a big business, there is a need for a more effective system of financial accountability. The treasurer has a key role to play.

Clarisse, aged 73, says she has always considered herself a leader. She was in a leadership position for 20 years in her job, and throughout those years she never stopped learning. In the latter years of her professional life, Clarisse taught law students about the court system and found teaching to be the most rewarding aspect of her job. Leadership to Clarisse means more than just having a responsible position, it means sharing knowledge and experience with others in a teaching role.

As a Justice of the Peace, she was highly regarded by everyone—the law, society, judges, and her staff: She says of that experience,

> I had a terrific memory, and I could remember all the cases. Lawyers and judges asked my advice—and they went by my opinion. They also asked me to organize the court chambers, and I did. I had that place running like a clock. I laid down all the rules, and I took away power from some of those lawyers. One of the judges used to say, "You run this place like God."

When Clarisse first joined Carnegie Hall, her "life was at a standstill." She had been forced to retire early when her daughter became terminally ill. She spent 2 years caring for her and lost all contact with other people. When her daughter died, she just wanted to be alone, and another 2 years went by before she realized she was desperately missing something: "I wasn't using my mind and I missed the activity of work. I had a great deal of professional responsibility, and when I retired, I did say 'Thank God' at first, but it wasn't long before I realized how much I missed it."

Clarisse joined the hiking group and soon felt that she was getting and not giving. She had always been a volunteer, even while working full time, and she felt she wanted to give Carnegie Hall whatever she had to offer. Regaining self-confidence after retirement has been a long process for her. She often felt like giving up, but says, "but something inside wouldn't let me." Clarisse has always had a strong drive to learn more about herself. She takes courses because she loves the challenge and excitement of learning. Her participation in the leadership program that Carnegie Hall offered enabled her to get in touch with her administrative skills, and after the confidence-building course, she assumed the role of treasurer. She finds great satisfaction in the work, and when people appreciate it, that is a plus. "Anyone who contributes something worthwhile is eventually recognized for their ability." As she relives her life experience, Clarisse becomes animated and increasingly self-assured.

Getting in touch with the influence and power she enjoyed in the past renews her confidence in her abilities and in her own power. In her current job as treasurer at Carnegie Hall, Clarisse is drawing on many of the skills developed so successfully in her professional life. Just as she reorganized the system in the court chambers, she is creating a system of financial reporting that will make the center run more efficiently. Furthermore, she is teaching that system to chairpersons of the activity groups. The following dialogue focuses on the development of a more efficient reporting system, and how to encourage all the activity groups to comply. Clarisse's sensitivity to volunteers and her facilitative approach is noteworthy, especially in contrast to the president's and the secretary's more directive style.

Director: *Madam Treasurer, would you like to talk about changes in the report forms for the chairpersons?*

Treasurer: *Yes, I have typed a little form on the back of their monthly reports for them to fill in their treasurer's report.*

President: *We've had problems with many of the groups. People come to me bitching about what's going on. Some say the money is invested. I would like this solved once and for all. We can set out a simple procedure. But we can tell them until we are blue in the face and they still won't listen.*

Director: *I think we have to be sensitive to the individual needs of the groups. Some groups have very small amounts of money, others have a large amount. We need to recognize the different kinds of accounts, too: for example, petty cash, membership, savings.*

President: *Don't you think a sermon is necessary?*

Director *No, I don't think so. Some groups just don't have bank accounts.*

Treasurer: *I think it would be helpful to have the same format for all the groups.*

Secretary: *What if some say no? I think the directives for change should come from us.*

Past President: *I think we need to say we are open and accountable with you and you need to be open and accountable with us. That's the beginning and the end of it.*

Treasurer: *I could see that the chairperson of the quilting group knew what she was doing. She didn't do it like a bookkeeper would do, but she isn't a bookkeeper, she is a volunteer, and she is doing the best she can. I think if we just get a system, it will help her, then the chairpersons will feel secure having a specific procedure to follow.*

It is 12:15 p.m., and deliberations have exceeded 2 hours without a break. Sighs of relief are audible as the meeting spills out into a busy lunch hour.

Noon Hour Lunch

According to Betty, aged 65, the hot lunch program is "the flagship program of the center.. . . Many seniors get a nutritious and inexpensive hot noon meal here that they would not otherwise have." The line for lunch today is particularly long. Few seem to mind the wait and pass the time in conversation. There are always exceptions. Anastasia, a notorious complainer, barges in front of the others, saying, "This is disgusting. Look at them there in the kitchen, cackling like a bunch of hens, just having a good time and making us wait. All they want is our money." A number of people, like Anastasia, come regularly for the hot meal and do not participate in any other programs. Some are bitter; some are alcoholic or drug-dependent. Although they may not make for the best lunch table conversation, they are nevertheless accepted in the center.

In the middle of each table are a small bouquet of fresh flowers and a sign in a clear plastic holder, developed in one of the educational workshops, reading

---

The Art of Lunchtime Chatter
Check how well you are doing:
1. I am pleasant.
2. I am positive.
3. I talk about problems.
4. I share the time so that each person has an opportunity to talk, listen and ask questions.
How well did you do?

Not everyone reads it.

It's 1:30 p.m. as about 40 people gather in the Oak Room for the monthly chairpersons meeting.

Chairpersons Meeting

Like the executive board meeting, the agenda for this meeting is set by the director, Jo-Ann, and the president, Margaret; however, Jo-Ann plays a minor role in this meeting, and Margaret is fully in charge. Final decisions about the operations of the center are made in this meeting. No initiative taken or decision made in the executive meeting can be implemented without ratification by chairpersons representing the membership of 34 activity groups. A certain sensitivity is required in advocating ideas, and in giving chairpersons a sense of autonomy and power in the decision-making process.

As the meeting begins, members of the board are seated along a head table, with a roomful of chairpersons facing them in rows. As at the executive meeting, people are dressed in business attire. It takes three raps of the gavel for the president to bring the meeting to order.

President: *I really needed to bang that gavel today. I am glad you're all so happy. Louis posted the minutes last week. Would someone please make a motion?*

Old Business

President: *In a whole week of checking memberships, we only found four people who weren't members, so we decided to continue doing random checks. Please tell your members not to be offended if they are asked to produce a membership card. With respect to guests, may I refer you to our policy and procedures manual, page 3.*

New Business

President: *I notice there are quite a few people missing today, and that's unfortunate. Please take all the information back to your groups. You have an agenda, make some notes on it, and when you go back to your groups, as you are knitting or quilting or whatever, tell your members about what goes on in the meeting. Clarisse, do you want to tell us how the new monthly financial reporting system works?*

Treasurer: *[She explains the system]: Any questions? If you want to set up the system, I'd be pleased to help you.*

The chairpersons then present their monthly reports, each report being formally motioned, seconded, and approved.

Activity Group Reports

Sick and Well Chairperson: *Good morning everyone. Last month I sent 12 cards. I'm sorry to report the passing of Gladys Jones. You are probably wondering what I did with that $30.00. I bought cards at $1.49 on sale today. Cash on hand again? Same as last month—nil.*

President: *Thank you, Irene, that's not as dismal as last month.*

Pottery Chairperson: *Well, we have 14 members, all busy and enthusiastic and making pots.*

Computer Club Chairperson: *I am the new kid on the block. I've been a member for 20 years, but I just got involved because I thought it was time to learn about bits and bites and all those things the grandchildren always talk about. We have nine members but we need more. We have 10 computer systems, and I have never seen anyone down there playing with them.*

Canasta Chairperson: *We are going along as usual. We have three tables of canasta, we met four times, and we have $8 for the association—I'm going to give it to you in nickels.*

Hikers' Chairperson: *Well, we particularly enjoyed last week's hike. We went back because we liked the birds; they were singing. And we are very pleased to report that we have three new men in our group.*

Quilting Chairperson: *We met 12 times with a total attendance for the month of 73. We welcomed a new member, Olga Wilson. Gertie has been away. One of our members has decided to retire. Cash on hand is $26.*

Dance Chairperson: *Last month 204 people danced from morning until afternoon. Our instructor's father died and we donated $30 to the heart fund.*

Walkers' Chairperson: *We walked four times and a total of 52 people participated. One Friday was a bit of a washout.*

Executive Board Reports

President: *We are missing a number of people. I guess I better change my deodorant. That's disappointing. There has been a lot of good discussion here. Some people will say we've railroaded things through. The groups should all be represented at these meetings.*

Past President: *I'm always impressed by the people who come out to these meetings each time and sit patiently. I think you are all doing a good job. Some of this is a little on the dry side. As a center we have a lot to be proud of. Now we are even up for nomination for an award. We've all been a part of it and we can all enjoy the fruits of our labors.*

President: *Last week we entertained the Mayor and the new director of the Seniors Bureau. We did this to develop good working relations and promote good will in the community.*

Treasurer: *I'd like to report on the mentoring program. The Minister of Education referred to the program in a recent speech as an example of how seniors are getting more involved in the community. In the fall, two students studied the court system, and this has expanded: two are mentoring computer work and two more are creating a habitat for snakes. Besides renewed interest in education, students are developing a close personal relationship with an older person. The future looks bright as more business and community groups get involved and make the connections with education and kids.*

President: *It's time to close. Anybody heard any good jokes?*

A chairperson leaps to her feet. "Have you heard about the woman who lost 160 pounds? She divorced her husband."

At 4:30 p.m. the music fades. Within minutes, the pianist, a 91-year-old woman less than 5 feet tall wearing a floral print dress and track shoes, exits from the piano room and charges the full length of the building, out the front door, and down the street.

☐ The Meaning of Life: Beliefs, Values, and Hidden Assumptions

What does this narrative reveal about the meaning of life at Carnegie Hall? It provides a flavor of the activities, conduct of business, characteristics and styles of leaders, and interactions between staff and seniors. The summary of the history, the center's policies, and the narrative account illuminate the deeper beliefs and values about the nature of retirement, the needs and capacities of seniors, power, and leadership.

The Nature of Retirement

The history of this center reflects a view of retired people as valued, having a certain status in the community, and, contrary to the disengagement theory of aging prominent when the center opened, wanting to remain a visible part of the community. The presence of wheelchairs and the structure of the environment provide clues that retirement may involve physical disabilities. Retirement also means aging, which for some has its negative aspects, such as problems with sore feet that can be alleviated by the resident podiatrist. But old age does not imply disengagement. (Although there are many disengaged and isolated old people, they will not be found in a seniors' center.)

The environment itself is a lively one, with senior volunteers welcoming people at the door, preparing and serving meals, selling raffle tickets, answering the telephone, serving as office assistants and receptionists, and managing the senior peer counseling office. However, the transition from work to a productive, volunteer role, was seldom smooth for most seniors. Many experienced retirement as premature and traumatic. If widowhood is considered a legitimate form of retirement, everyone experienced the loss of a primary role as undesired, with no direction or expectation for the future. Margaret, Betty, and Marilyn were let go from work before they were 65; Louis was forced to retire early for health reasons; Clarisse retired to care for her daughter; Florence, Liz, Evelyn, and Fred did not lose jobs prematurely but lost spouses with whom they anticipated spending their retirement years. During the early postretirement phase, many experienced depression, physical disability, or both and one person spoke of being suicidal. They all related feeling isolated, missing social contact, and needing a focus. Aging is about fire and rebirth. It is about sustaining passion about someone or something and constantly being reborn when one's breath is taken away after each loss that occurs (Taganyaki, 1997).

The experience of these seniors is consistent with Bengston and Kuyper's cycle of social breakdown (cited in Payne, 1977), which involves a critical period of disengagement from work, followed by a loss of self-esteem and self-confidence, and which is often associated with a deterioration of physical and mental health, and social isolation. It lends support to Matthews and Brown's (1987) findings that attitude and choice are key factors in whether one experiences retirement negatively. For those who are forced to retire prematurely, the opportunity for involvement in voluntary leadership roles can serve as a replacement for work, reducing the negative impact of retirement.

It was not, however, the need to get involved and find a replacement for work that initially prompted the nine seniors interviewed to join a seniors' center. They said they missed the social contact and the stimulation related to employment and sought social contact in a seniors' center, even though they did not see themselves as old, as they did the rest of the people there. As one woman said, "When I was working, I had contact with people 8 hours a day. When I retired, I wasn't willing to give up. Here I get a sense of continuity with people still buzzing around." The function of the center is primarily social: people referred to it as a "home away from home" and a "comfortable place to be"—a refuge from "loneliness and inactivity." This warmth and acceptance is something seniors seldom find in the outside world. One person remarked, "Carnegie Hall is a place where seniors are valued . . . but more than that it is very personal. People in the outside world are all geared up for themselves and they aren't particularly interested in your problems." It was not very long before they felt connected to other people. It was not so much that they had acquired intimate friends, but that they were recognized and felt a sense of acceptance and belonging.

Carnegie Hall also functions as a springboard to other involvements in the community. A member remarked, "Everything is possible that could launch you to someplace else." Some take a strong leadership role in promoting intergenerational exchanges between the senior choir and schoolchildren. Other are enthusiastic about a mentoring program that link schoolchildren who are at risk with seniors in the community. These seniors are not only contributing the skills and abilities of a lifetime to the center and the broader community, they are also changing negative attitudes toward older people as less active and able—attitudes that are commonly held by younger people and seniors themselves.

Carnegie Hall offers seniors an opportunity to engage in volunteer roles that provide a certain role continuity, social support, satisfaction, and self-esteem. It provides an opportunity to contribute to the community in creative and imaginative ways that can be more enjoyable and enriching than one's past work or family role.

Who are the retired people that Carnegie Hall services? The movers and shakers and the old folks are fully integrated into the culture; people no longer see the distinction between themselves and "old people." One senior remarked, "We are all members and no one thinks he or she is old." What everyone receives at Carnegie Hall that is not readily available to retired people in society, is acceptance and belonging in a safe and comfortable environment. Given the number of recreational programs and activities, and the people who come for lunch or activities and do not volunteer, the general assumption about retirement seems to be that it is a time to relax and have fun, and seniors' centers exist to provide this service.

For senior leaders, however, retirement is a time to continue developing their personal potential and to make a contribution to the community to the end of life. And for some, given health, self-confidence, and opportunity, it is the time of their life. This would not seem to be an expectation commonly shared in the center. The questions are, What needs does such involvement serve? and, What kinds of need satisfaction influences the development of leadership potential?

Needs of Seniors

Marilyn, a member of Carnegie Hall, describes the center as

> a place for making wishes and dreams come true—perhaps secret dreams and wishes that could not be fulfilled earlier in life. Now that one is a senior and has time, anything seems possible. Carnegie Hall provides many of these possibilities and opportunities. A chance to sing, dance, be artistic, learn new things, and meet new people. No talent or qualifications required: the sky's the limit.

Older people in society are typically viewed as having needs, yet seldom are their abilities or potentials or dreams identified or given expression. Acknowledging the desires and aspirations of older people is not part of the social service mandate throughout North America that has given rise to a plethora of services for the retired, such as municipally subsidized leisure services.

A number of basic needs associated with aging can be served at a center. The environment is designed to accommodate physical disabilities, policy promotes social and health care services, and history and policy both attest to a wide range of recreational programs from the more traditional crafts and bingo, to ceramics, hiking, and travel. Current policy is to satisfy "leisure and social and educational needs of senior adults: and to provide an environment where members feel positive self-worth through acceptance by others, belonging, recognition, contribution, and achievement." Increasingly, educational programs such as the Mental Fitness Program (Cusack & Thompson, 1998), satisfy some of the higher order needs for achievement, personal development, creative expression, and influence and contribution, and maintain a level of power and control enjoyed during working years.

The center offers unconditional acceptance: every person is valued for who he or she is. Inherent is the assumption that people, when they retire, leave the past behind and become more equal. This represents a dilemma for those who want to continue to develop their skills and potentials in retirement. One person said,

> The difference between the working world and retirement is that in the working world you are accepted for what you do and in retirement you are accepted for who you are. But who you are includes what you have done in the past; who you are now and what you can do; and who you will become in the future.

While senior leaders talked about their social needs and their need for acceptance, they also talked about their desires and aspirations, indicating that they wanted to make a contribution to the community. They also said they are motivated by a challenge and the opportunity to learn new things about themselves and others.

When they were encouraged to talk about their leadership skills, however, they had more difficulty acknowledging strengths than weaknesses. Although they could admit they had skills and talents developed over a lifetime, they spoke repeatedly of losing self-esteem and self-confidence as a consequence of retirement. For many of these people, the educational programs provided a forum for people to discuss their past achievements and to be recognized for what they had done, enhancing their self-esteem and self-confidence.

Certainly many influences in any organization prompt people to take on a leadership role, and an important one at Carnegie Hall is the director's belief in the skills and potential of seniors. A request from the director to assume a leadership role often provided the confidence to take a risk and make a commitment. Jo-Ann believes in the skills and abilities of members and knows that the center benefits when these skills are put to use. She takes an interest in each person and is sensitive to an individual's needs. Many said they had taken on a leadership role because the director (or her assistant, the programmer) had made a specific request. A simple, well-timed invitation often initiated the process of developing individual seniors as leaders. In describing how volunteering made them feel, they used words like *uplifted, useful, satisfied, more confident, exhilarated, bouncy, proud, appreciated, energetic,* and *10-feet tall*. With few exceptions, when they agreed to commit themselves they never imagined just how enriching the experience would be.

Power

The philosophy of leadership is to put seniors in charge of the opera-tions—that is, to *empower* them. The question, Who really holds the power? is a challenging one. When asked, seniors initially expressed a view that either the president, the director, or both had the power. This is consistent with the hierarchical organizational structure (The flow chart in Figure 1 places the director and president nearby and at the same level, whereas the executive board is much lower on the page. Such details have subtle effects on perceptions of power.) Policy also suggests that the president and director share the power (e.g., those decisions not dealt with in the meetings are returned to the director and president for consid-eration). On an individual level, everyone at Carnegie Hall has a certain amount of power, should they choose to exercise it, simply because the staff and executive board are there to ensure that member needs are being met. As Jo-Ann describes it,

> Anyone who engages in the conversation has power. People have as much power as they want to have, and to the level that they are involved, or make their needs and wants known. The man who walks in quietly (no one knows his name), plays cards, and never says boo, probably doesn't have any power. But if he or she comes in screaming and hollering about the parking lot, then someone is going to listen.

Ultimately, it is the director's responsibility to listen, see what the concern is, and see that it is resolved.

The executive board has power because it represents the membership, but it does not make all the decisions. The cooperation of membership, staff, and executive board is the key factor. Jo-Ann and the staff manage the day-to-day operations, put programs in place, and work with the executive board to meet the needs of the membership. As Jo-Ann re-marked,

> Staff are here for the members. There are expectations of both of staff and executive, and when one lets the other down, we all suffer. The staff is a small team and the board is a small team. Together we run the show, but in the final analysis, it is the members who do.

Some decisions are the responsibility of the board and some the responsibility of staff. For example, Jo-Ann and the staff make many of the decisions regarding maintenance. In the executive meeting, everyone comes with issues for discussion. Some decisions are the board's, some are the staff's, some are the chairpersons', and some are made within the activity groups.

The director, staff, president, and executive board work to maintain the autonomy of the groups and to enable the participation of activity group members in decision-making processes. Participation in decision making fosters ownership, pride, and a sense of individual responsibility that filters through the ranks. The groups and each individual feel empowered by the process. At the same time, the process acts as a check and balance, as well as a way of communicating information to the membership. If the executive board obtains support for an idea at the chairpersons meeting, they feel reassured that they are reflecting what the members really want and need.

Jo-Ann believes in the power of the membership and her desire to transfer power to seniors; she claims that all members have as much power as they choose to exercise. Many seniors were reluctant to acknowledge they had power. These assumptions about power and authority as well as deeply held beliefs about their own powerlessness in a group act as barriers, preventing people from having a greater share of influence and power in the center.

Every board experiences challenges relating to power and personal conflict. When there are differences of opinion, people are often reluctant to speak up. Asked why they do not exercise their power and speak up when there is frustration or conflict, board members said they wanted to avoid resentment and hurting people's feelings. In being silent, some said they were not giving their power away, but rather choosing to wait for the right opportunity or showing respect for the other person's right to an opinion. Others said they keep quiet when they know they are right. And as Fred said, "Some things are just not important enough to be bothered with. If people go on a power trip, well I guess they need to."

When conflict and tension arise in meetings, there is a loss of energy in the group. After one of the meetings, everyone admitted to being exhausted. In contrast, the mood in another of the chairpersons meetings was more light-hearted, the discussion more lively. People had come prepared to participate, were more actively engaged, and said they felt exhilarated after the meeting.

When one person assumes too much responsibility and dominates a meeting, others are robbed of their power and their energy depleted. Draining energy is a subtle process, and throwing in a joke at the end of a meeting is not enough. When people share the problems and the power, more energy is available and everyone enjoys an enhanced feeling of accomplishment and well-being. The connection between energy and power is seldom made, however, and senior leaders tend to give their power and energy to people who take charge of meetings. (Practical information for leaders on how to generate group energy is provided in Chapter 8.)

Many seniors, and certainly most who attend seniors' centers (i.e., predominantly women), have had little power in their working lives. Although many have had influence and power in their homes and families, they tend not to derive a sense of power that transfers to other settings. Furthermore, they often hold a view of power as negative, involving authority and control over others. And although everyone may wish to remain in control of their personal lives, most have difficulty seeing themselves as having a measure of power over their peers.

Issues and assumptions about gender are related to power and leadership. Many retirement organizations are dominated by women, and women are equitably represented in positions of power. Curiously, with the exception of the past president, the only man on the board serves as secretary. And he expressed feelings of frustration and of being robbed of his power. On another occasion, a chairperson closed the meeting with a sexist joke at the expense of the men. Men rarely attend educational or training programs. However, women seldom see themselves as leaders in the traditional sense of the word. Sexism and gender warfare take on new meaning in Centennial Center, portrayed in Chapter 5.

Leadership

Leadership is relational, and although influence flows throughout the organization, it is in the relationship between the executive (particularly the president) and the director that we see how leadership functions and how power is shared. This involves the professional leader and senior leader having particular skills and approaches to accomplishing the tasks of the center—skills that balance and complement each other.

The director is confident in her leadership skills and is not afraid to speak up about sensitive issues. Jo-Ann does not avoid conflict, always carries a task to completion, and is prepared to confront people, while realizing that sensitivity is required. She is always prepared for meetings. With both staff and seniors, her focus is on challenging and inspiring people.

Jo-Ann is also fully aware of what she does that influences seniors to get more involved. She states, "Everything depends on attitude. If you have the right attitude with people and you enjoy them, then you can be a motivator." She makes leadership easier for seniors. Leadership can have different connotations, and she tries to encourage them to see the benefits and opportunities. Jo-Ann goes on to say, "I like to make sure that when they win, they win big—and if they don't, I make sure they aren't going to fall flat on their face. Staff and executive are there to give support and recognition. The key is knowing people well and understanding their individual needs and talents. Jo Ann reflects,

> Staff take the time to get to know people, their level, their interests. The sense of recognition, success, and belonging that people get from being involved are personal things that people appreciate. The secret is to find out what are the keys for people, what is it that hooks them.

The style of leadership Jo-Ann exemplifies is one that Barth (1991) typified as instrumental in developing a community of leaders. She creates a climate in which seniors emerge as leaders, sometimes for the first time in retirement. She is also a strong advocate of the value of education in developing leadership potential, and she admits that staff cannot provide the sophisticated approach, because they have neither the time nor expertise to train people. They do, however, try to remove barriers to participation and leadership, and to assist seniors in identifying training needs. Jo-Ann describes the appraoch:

> If people identify needs then we can use those needs as a bulwark to remove the problems. We may initiate some suggestions and then seniors begin to generate their own. And if we can find out where to get funds, then we help people to get the needed training programs in place.

As a result of leadership and personal development programs, Carnegie Hall now has many more skilled leaders. However, many of the deeper beliefs and assumptions about power, leadership, and their own abilities and capacities still prevent many leaders from exercising their influence and sharing the power, and this in turn prevents others from becoming involved and emerging as leaders.

☐ What the Story Tells Us About Empowering Seniors

The story of Carnegie Hall provides rich insights into how to empower seniors and how to share the leadership in seniors' groups and organizations. When people share the leadership, they share power. Empowerment has *power* as its root word: It literally means giving or sharing power. According to the dictionary, empowerment has two aspects to its definition: (1) to give legitimate authority (i.e., power) to make a decision, or perform a role, and (2) to enable people to exercise that authority.

Empowerment means creating legitimate opportunities for seniors to take more responsibility for decision making at a level they can handle and giving them the tools (e.g., training, strength, energy, knowledge, skills) to carry out those responsibilities effectively. In the retirement community of professionals and seniors, the following is agreed:

1. Giving legitimate authority and opportunity translates to:

• Responsibilities outlined in policy guide
• Authority recognized and understood by all
• No hidden agendas

2. Enabling people to exercise authority or assume responsibility means:

• Making sure training is available
• Serving people's needs
• Recognizing their strengths and talents
• Motivating and inspiring
• Supporting and encouraging
• Extending opportunities for gradual involvement
• Building confidence and self-esteem
• Developing understanding of how the organization works
• Building skills of effective leadership in retirement
• Recognizing their achievements
• Challenging and stimulating
• Creating empowering relationships

Carnegie Hall offers retired people unconditional acceptance and visibility. It supports a view of retirement as a time for active involvement and continued contribution in self-chosen endeavors—a time to offer one's skills and talents and to continue to develop them to the end of life. To develop a meaningful role for themselves, seniors require help in refining existing skills and, in many cases, developing new ones. A style of leadership that focuses on supporting and developing the potential of people contributes to the emergence of seniors as leaders.

What must happen for more seniors to become involved in sharing leadership and power in seniors' organizations and in benefiting from the rich rewards that accompany such involvement? The tale of Carnegie Hall suggests how assumptions about retirement, the needs of seniors, and the nature of power and leadership serve as strong barriers to emergent leaders. Educational opportunities play an important role in changing the assumptions, developing leadership skills, and the level of self-confidence and self-esteem needed to participate more fully in community life.

Chapter 5 tells a different story of a seniors' center that serves as a model of traditional leadership in a retirement organization. Once again, the narrative illuminates how leadership works and provides deep insights into the meaning and value of activities and relationships. Surprising insights into gender differences in attitudes and expressions of power and approaches to leadership are revealed.

5
CHAPTER

Centennial Center: Portraits of Power and What We Can Learn

> The measure of leadership is not the quality of the head, but the tone of the body. The signs of outstanding leadership appear primarily among the group members. Are members reaching their potential? Are they learning? Serving? . . . Do they change with grace? Manage conflict?
> —De Pree, M., 1987, p. 11, 12

This chapter portrays another seniors' center in a neighboring city of approximately 80,000 people. The center is referred to as Centennial Center because the last renovations of it coincided with centennial celebrations, making it a state-of-the-art seniors' center. Although its physical structure and service delivery, luxurious bowling green, and exemplary rose garden may be state of the art, leadership operates in the center according to an organizational effectiveness approach that may work in some organizations but does not work in retirement organizations. The center thus serves as an example of organizations around the world that experience the effects of traditional authoritarian leadership. The problems inherent in authoritarian leadership (e.g., a desperate need for volunteers, difficulty finding effective leaders, a number of people —primarily women—who do not speak their views, nostalgia for the good old days when people mattered more, constant conflict and frustration) are illustrated here. As in Chapter 4, this chapter begins with a

100

historical perspective. An outline of the organizational structure follows. The chapter concludes with a discussion both of the deeper values and assumptions commonly held by community members and of what the narrative illustrates regarding power, conflict, and the battle of the sexes. Again, organizations are dynamic systems that are constantly changing, and like a photograph, this portrait of the center represents a moment frozen in time.

☐ A Place for Seniors

Centennial Center's history is brief because it has been in operation for only 15 years. Although no formal history exists, an oral history was pieced together from those who have been affiliated with the center from the beginning. Like the surrounding community, the history of the center is characterized by rapid population growth, similar to communities everywhere that are simultaneously experiencing dramatic growth and population aging. The actual number of people over 50 years of age (i.e., those eligible to join a seniors' center) is comparable with the community in which Carnegie Hall is located. However, the total population of the community in which Centennial Center is located has increased ten-fold in the past 60 years, whereas that surrounding Carnegie Hall has only doubled. In a climate of rapid growth coupled with economic recession, seniors in Centennial Center are fighting for visibility and competing for scarce tax dollars.

☐ In the Beginning . . .

In the early years, dinner dances were a popular activity, and the work was shared by the members and a staff of three. About 125 people usually attended the dinner dances: people were asked to bring a covered dish, and they would lay out a potluck smorgasbord. As the membership grew, the Health Department became involved and ruled that because of health regulations, members should not be bringing food from home. The staff then assumed sole responsibility for preparing and cooking food for the dinner dances. One staff member recalled, "We'd have a salmon barbecue and hose off the scales out on the lawn. Then we'd be washing pots and pans. When I look back, I don't know how we did it. Hard work, but a lot of fun." Many people shared this nostalgia for the good old days and admitted a feeling that things were better then. Staff and members worked together as a team, and staff always had time for the members.

One staff member attributes the difference between the good old days and the present to the size of the center and the level of education required to run it. One staff member remarked,

> It's more like a business around here. I hated to see the last addition [to the building]: it put us over the edge. There is a big difference in the staff and the way they do their jobs. Often they stay in their offices. Others are so busy they don't have time to talk to people. I don't blame anyone. We are all overworked.

A perception shared by many older members was that the rapid growth in membership reflected increasing numbers of younger people (i.e., those aged 50 to 65 years) taking advantage of the wide range of low-cost educational courses and the athletic programs. Currently, there are more than 3000 members, with 9 staff employees who assist in programming, registration, food services, and overall operation of the center. From the beginning the center has had a strong sports program (e.g., curling, lawn bowling, snooker) as well as traditional crafts, woodworking, and musical groups. Community support services that hold their meetings in the center include an arthritis support group, a blood pressure clinic, a stroke club, a cardiac rehabilitation program, a widows group, and a caregivers support group.

Educational courses are increasingly part of the center's activities. A lecture series addresses various topics, including "A Closer Look at Religion," the Arab-Israeli conflict, self-esteem, meditation, and "Philosophy: The Art of Wonder I (Introduction to Philosophy)." Computer classes are increasingly popular, and computing enthusiasts are involved in programming decisions and the operation of classes, and serve as teachers and teaching assistants.

☐   Profile of Professional Leadership

Alison (a pseudonym), the coordinator since 1977, has provided strong leadership and continuity in the evolution of programs and services. She is described as a powerful woman by both members and staff.

Alison's mission was to help seniors think young, leave the work ethic behind, and enjoy their retirement years. She regrets that it is increasingly difficult to maintain personal relationships with members, although, she says, "I always make a point of greeting people by name." With the growth of the center and increase in staff, her role has become increasingly administrative.

Because of growing membership and lack of time for the staff to socialize, the coordinator has instituted a hostess program. She says of this program, "The role of the hostesses is to welcome people and this is where the women play a leadership role in the center. Women like helping with the hostess program—they get to dress up—whereas the men just don't feel comfortable in the role. She encourages staff and hostesses to do walkabouts and to be as accessible as possible to members. She also encourages them to socialize in the beverage areas and to facilitate connections among people—especially to introduce members to the leaders of activities they may be interested in joining. Alison describes the center's current needs as follows:

> We need more volunteers. Some older people have a real fear of making a commitment because they are retired and they worry that volunteer responsibilities might interfere with holidays: many go to California in the winter months. Others are reluctant if their health is not good because they feel if they get ill, they won't be able to carry things out. Certainly, there is a greater reticence on the part of women.

Alison adds, however, that as soon as people have had the freedom to relax and enjoy themselves in their early retirement years, they often want to become involved in something more productive and meaningful. That is when she finds ways to make use of their unique skills and talents to serve the needs of the center. She is hopeful that the upcoming leadership-training program will prepare seniors to undertake formal leadership roles that will make others feel welcome and become more involved in the center.

☐ Organizational Structure

The *Advisory Board Policy and Procedures Manual* defines the formal structure of power relations and the roles of key people in the center. The first item in the constitution is the mandate of the center:

> To promote within the limitations of allocated resources year-round opportunities for satisfying the leisure needs of senior adults in this community over the age of 50. As well, to provide information services for senior adults whenever possible.

> To be a community focal point on aging where older persons can come together for services and activities, as well as a community resource for information on aging.

> To provide settings in which members may experience acceptance by others, the feeling of belonging and recognition as individuals of positive worth.

Despite a detailed list of program objectives, including encouraging seniors "to use their own initiative in developing and leading programs,"

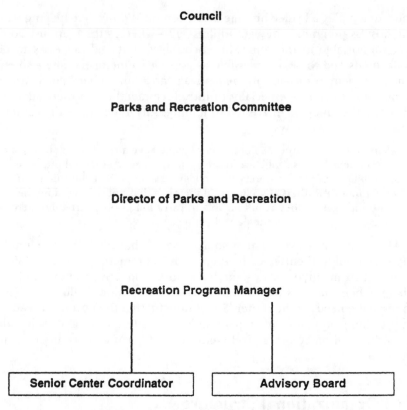

FIGURE 1.   Internal and external organizational structure of power in Centennial Center.

and the provision of "education/information" programs, no reference is made to leadership training or the development of seniors as leaders.

The second item in the constitution outlines power relations. The formal structure of authority is outlined in Figure 1. (The flow chart emphasizes external power and suggests that, within the center, power is shared between the coordinator and the board.)

The city council grants authority to the coordinator, who works with an advisory board and the activity committees. The coordinator attends all advisory board meetings as a nonvoting executive secretary and is charged with informing the board if any of its recommendations are not in accordance with district policies. If the board wishes to recommend a policy change, it can request that recommendations be forwarded to the council.

The advisory board is defined as a representative group of senior adults who voluntarily assist and advise the Center Coordinator regarding program direction of Centennial Center, program being the sum total of all that individuals do in the name of the Center. Potential members of the Advisory Board will be given a copy of the Advisory Board terms of reference—as ratified by Council Resolution no. 1324—so that they are in full understanding of their role and can agree to serve as a member in the outlined capacity.

The role of advisory board members is outlined as follows:

- To assist in identification and assessment of needs and desires of senior adults
- To act as a sounding board for suggested ideas and new programs from members and coordinator
- To make recommendations relative to program development
- To promote the center throughout the community
- To encourage involvement and attendance by all seniors
- To identify problems which cause tension and recommend solutions
- To make recommendations regarding fund raising

The advisory board consists of nine voting members: a president, vice-president, treasurer, crafts director, cultural director, sports director, social and educational director, and a past president (as well as the nonvoting coordinator, serving in the role of executive secretary). The four directors are liaisons with the various activity groups, conducting joint meetings with elected chairpersons from their respective groups to discuss common business as well as individual group needs and concerns. All board positions are elected annually, and the president and vice-president are elected at the annual general meeting.

The business of the advisory board is conducted at meetings held once a month. An executive committee (consisting of the president, vice-president, treasurer, past president, executive secretary, and two finance directors) meets as needed, with authority vested by the advisory board, and are charged with providing formal reports of such meetings at subsequently scheduled advisory board meetings.

☐ Membership Profile

The constitution provides detailed regulations regarding membership. All seniors participating in center activities must become members on or before their third visit. The ratio of women to men in Centennial Center is 3 to 2. The men, however, are more visible and considerably more active in leadership roles. As Alison describes it,

Women chair committees and activity groups, but few women serve on the advisory board. Generally, the women think that men should have their say. Men, on the other hand, come in and want to be in charge. Snooker and bridge just aren't satisfying enough for many of them.

☐ Welcome to Centennial Center

It is 8:40 a.m. as a new member approaches Centennial Center which lies at the heart of a maze of community services—a skating rink, public library, track, tennis courts, lawn bowling green, public health clinic, social recreation center, swimming pool, and a senior secondary school are within a three-block radius. On her way to the main entrance of a modern, one-story building, she passes a large, immaculately groomed lawn bowling green. The grass is so short and green she can hardly believe it is real. Freshly painted white benches at the edge of a circular path surround the green, with a traditional green clubhouse trimmed in white on the far side. Between the green and the center lies a rose garden, with numerous varieties marked with their proper names, arbors, and winding paths leading to a dais with a side entrance to the center.

It is 8:50 a.m. as she approaches the double-wide glass doors to Centennial Center. With a burst of air, the doors fly open automatically and she finds herself, like Alice in *Through the Looking Glass,* in a large atrium with a long glass case lining the left side that holds athletic trophies. A display of photographs mounted on cardboard runs the full length of the glass case and announces, "Congratulations to all Senior Games Competitors," with a list of all those competitors from Centennial Center who came home with silver, bronze, or gold medals.

Alison, the coordinator of the center has many responsibilities. Her role includes managing a staff of nine, as well as supervising and budgeting the overall operations of a center serving a diverse membership of more than 3000 people. She defines the primary function of the center as a social one and her primary role as a facilitator of socialization. She claims, "Recreation and activities are just the vehicles for socialization." She also admits that the center is a big business, although she had not thought of it that way until the president brought it to her attention.

Alison believes leadership is different in retirement. The major difference, she says, is in the approach to accomplishing things and the way in which work is delegated: "You just don't delegate seniors to do things. As a woman, I don't like that kind of supervision, and staff don't either. So I like to have a team approach." Involving seniors is different; they are volunteers, and using volunteer resources is different than supervising paid staff. In working with volunteers, she says, "You need the personal approach. You have to know what motivates people, what interests them, and where their strengths lie. I ask people and I like to kind of lead them along the path that they don't know they want to go [down] until they have had a chance to talk about it."

She finds it a challenge and is creative in making use of people's skills and talents to meet the needs of the center. She observes, for example,

> We need to get more of an ethnic understanding here, because the ethnic mix in the community has increased. We have a new member from Hong Kong who is a cartographer. She told me about the various places around the world that she has lived and worked, and she said she could bring a multiethnic perspective to the center. And I immediately thought, "How am I going to tap into her?"

Alison is pleased, although puzzled, that so many people have signed up for the leadership-training program who are not in formal leadership roles at the center, and some are people she does not know.

George (aged 78), the president, is proud of the center and has dedicated himself to making it the best of its kind. He joined Centennial Center to find an outlet for his ambitions; he did not come for the athletic programs and is not interested in recreational pursuits. He had climbed to the top of the ladder in medical administration and he wanted to see if he might have an interest in climbing the ladder in a seniors' center. He finds chairing a hospital board no different than being president of a seniors' center. (George uses the organizational effectiveness approach: he brings a style of leadership developed throughout his working life in medical and social service administration to his work at Centennial Center.)

In the role of president, George has enjoyed meeting new people and has had an opportunity to achieve some of his goals in improving the operations of the organization. He remarks of his experience,

> It's a challenge. Like this morning. I heard about the snooker meeting after I got here. I asked the snooker people if it was publicized, and they said there was a notice on the board in the snooker room, and I said, "Well, supposing I don't go into the snooker room because I don't belong to the snooker club, how would I know about it?" And he said, "Don't ask me, and I said, "Well, I am asking you." You need to put a notice up where everybody can see it. These kinds of things go on and they shouldn't because it's half-baked. This whole place is a challenge because it is this funny mixture of different things happening and different people who are all set in their ways like me because they are aging.

In reflecting on his leadership qualities, George says he is critical of himself and others, is honest and consistent, and has a passion for resolving problems even when he gains no personal benefit. Confidence was never an issue for George: he admits that "probably I am too bold."

Annual General Meeting

The first days of summer in Olympia are hot and steamy. On one of these days, approximately 225 members assemble in the comfort of an air-conditioned gymnasium for the annual general meeting. The most common code of dress is California north—casual clothes and sneakers. Staff and advisory board members are distinguished by their business-like attire. When the advisory board members are seated at a long table across the stage, the meeting begins promptly at 1:00 p.m.

This meeting is George's swan song, his last official duty as president of the association, and he is comfortable, articulate, and fully in-charge of the proceedings. He brings the meeting to order with a moment's silence for "people we have lost in the last while," followed by the welcome and an outline of the agenda. The coordinator is then introduced and presents highlights of the year. The coordinator is upbeat and emphasizes cooperation and recognition that the center and staff are busier. The vice-president highlights the conflict with students in the parking lot. Seniors are fighting for their space in the community. (There is also evidence of sexist remarks and behavior: women on staff are lined up to be kissed by the vice-president.)

Coordinator: *We have a new relationship that epitomizes the spirit of cooperation here at Centennial Center. Our beautiful rose garden is a joint effort between the city and the center: the city planted the rose garden, and a group of our members who are rose enthusiasts look after the maintenance. Because our center is getting larger and staff are busier, we are taking steps to maintain a warm and friendly atmosphere. With this in mind, we have two new programs, the hostess program and Operation Friendship, that are designed to help new members feel welcome. We have also hired two leadership-training consultants, and you'll be hearing more about plans for a training program.*

Advisory Board Reports

Each member of the advisory board presents their report for the year. The vice-president begins. His report includes an important issue of great concern to all.

Vice-president: *Ladies and gentlemen, we have a parking problem. Students who attend the senior secondary school across the street are using our parking lot. We have applied to council for a permit to prevent the students from parking here. I will be here at 7:30 in the morning on the first day of school in September taking a list of students parked here. The students are going to learn the hard way that they can't park in our parking lot. [Loud cheering and clapping]*

Sports Director: *I have 2 minutes to report on 17 activities. We had a total of 650 participants in the following activities: slow-pitch, snooker, tennis, table tennis, golf, bocce, lawn bowling, carpet bowling, five-pin bowling, roller skating, ice skating, walking, hiking, biking. There is something for everyone, so let's get out there. Besides being fun, it's good for you.*

Crafts Director: *I don't like speaking in public, so please bear with me. I'm going to start off with the opposite sex. The boys in the woodworking shop have helped us a lot in the craft shop. Last year, they made all the horseshoes for the senior games. This is a quote that I can't pass up. One of the boys in the shop said, "The carpenter's shop is the most beautiful place in town: it's full of good looking, sexy old men.' The craft room is also a wonderful place. We meet twice a week, and we produce some lovely items. I want to give special thanks to Olga for her beautiful work. The gift shop is very successful this year. We sold both summer and seniors' games shirts and hats and we got 10% of the proceeds. The spring fair was the best ever and we made over $1000. We now have our very own Centennial Center t-shirts, also crests and caps. It would be nice to see you all wearing them and promoting our center. There is something very rewarding about volunteering. I have really enjoyed it*

President: *My years as president have been very enjoyable in spite of some personal problems, and this last year has been the best. Things don't just happen here, they occur because of the hard work of volunteers.*

Special Recognitions

President: *I would ask the coordinator and staff to step out here and get snowed under with flowers and affection. Vice-president, are you good at hugging? (Nine young women step onto the stage, each receiving a bouquet of flowers and a kiss from the vice-president.) We love you all. We need you. We hope you are here for a long time.*

Elections

This year a new member has been nominated for president, challenging the vice-president for the position. (This is further evidence of a competitive approach to leadership typical of the workplace and the political arena, but inappropriate to retirement organizations.) Both candidates address the assembly briefly:

Vice-president: *I joined this center to play snooker and I got interested and helped in the kitchen. I got a new table for the snooker club. I brought ideas for making improvements to the kitchen and they were defeated, but that's democracy. Anything I have done, I have done for the good of the people.*

Challenge Candidate: *I have been a member less than a year and since nominated, I have prepared a brief resume of my qualifications. I have been married for 50 years, have children and grandchildren. I have been a business administrator, and I was president of a large seniors' center in Montreal with a membership of over 4000. When I moved to Olympia this year I joined this center, and I urge you to vote for me.*

Someone from the floor calls for a secret ballot. In due course, the vice-president is declared the new President of Centennial Center and the meeting concludes with his acceptance speech, and final words: "thank you for the confidence in me. I will say this: as of the third week in September, the parking problem will be solved" (cheers). (His acceptance speech seems rather like a call to battle that begins with his first official day in office.)

From a chair strategically tucked in the corner just inside the glass doors to the seniors' center, Edward, the new president, in a Centennial Center sports cap and t-shirt with nose pressed against the glass, scrutinizes the parking lot, checking for incoming teens in cars. Behind him, a sign announces the upcoming Canadian Constitutional Debate to be held at the center.

Edward (aged 63) retired at age 55 from the federal government and has "never looked back." He joined Centennial Center, he says, to

> get out of my wife's hair. I was interested in snooker and I knew there was a very active snooker group. Through snooker, I found out how the board worked. I wasn't really satisfied with the way the kitchen was being run. When I asked what I could do about these problems, it was suggested that if I really wanted to change things, I should join the advisory board.

Edward gets satisfaction out of "taking the bull by the horns and deciding on things that have to be decided upon." He is not interested in physical sports; he gets enjoyment out of sitting in a meeting for 2 or 3 hours, sinking his teeth into a problem, and finding solutions. He finds it somewhat frustrating, however, that the board does not have more power. He describes his leadership as

> not really dogmatic, but I like to run what I call a straight and narrow meeting. If people have something to say, they raise their hands, and I

recognize them. As far as I am concerned, if you have the floor, everybody should listen. I like to run a meeting where business is attended to: the odd bit of humor is okay, but I like order. If two or three people are chatting, I would say, "Hey, let's attend to business." Nobody can say Edward doesn't give people equal opportunity.

It is 8:50 a.m. and the monthly advisory board meeting is scheduled to begin at 9:00. It is the first meeting of the new board, and Edward is in charge. He extends a particularly warm welcome to the new vice-president, Theresa, who is the former president of the funding society. She agreed to take on the role of vice-president because "they said, 'you really should.' They didn't know who else they were going to get, and . . . I felt duty-bound. I felt I owed Centennial Center: it really saved my husband and me, too. Don't misunderstand me, I'm more than glad to help." She never knows what she is going to get out of it when she assumes a responsible role but knows that she always gets more out of things than she puts in. She describes herself as confident and attributes her confidence to working out of the home.

Theresa believes that being a leader in retirement is much different from leading younger groups: "It doesn't matter so much how well you do it. It's a case of, 'I will do the best I can and so what.' I used to be terrified to make mistakes and I just laugh it off now." Although an effective leader has to be tolerant and understanding of people, regardless of the age group involved, she knows from experience that many seniors lack confidence. Many are desperate to join in, but they may stand back and wait to be invited and encouraged. Theresa is not prepared to say that women would necessarily make the best leaders. It would depend, she says, on the personality of the individual. I think a leader has to be kind and friendly and understand other people. Leaders must truly feel they are serving others, rather than being served in their leadership role."

Power has a negative connotation for Theresa, and she is not interested in having any of it. She admits that the coordinator is powerful but also kind and tolerant. Although she has observed that the coordinator, Alison, can stand her ground when needed, Theresa does not think she enjoys having to use that power.

Theresa is frustrated by people who complain often and try to stir up trouble. She encourages people who complain to participate in the decision-making process and to work toward consensus. Generally, issues are resolved and people are asked to settle down or leave.

The real challenge is finding volunteers. Everywhere she goes, the same people are always involved. Theresa claims that whether people volunteer depends to some extent on the way they were brought up: "I was brought up in a home where my mother was always involved in the church and doing things in the community. I grew up in the Depression years and things were tough, but people helped each other." Volunteers must have the desire to become involved and use their skills, which vary depending on the task. The center's responsibility is to provide the opportunity to develop those skills, with some fun and enjoyment built in. Theresa admits that some jobs just are not any fun, but someone has to do them. One way to find people to work in the kitchen is to say, "We'll close it down if nobody volunteers." One of the biggest reasons people are reluctant to take on responsibilities, in Theresa's view, has to do with lack of confidence. There must be a way for people to build their self-confidence, and she hopes that the leadership-training program will help.

It is 9:03 a.m. when the advisory board meeting is brought to order. (The coordinator's role changes to executive secretary at the advisory board meetings, suggesting that although she is in charge of the center as coordinator, in these meetings she has less power as secretary. Again, the business focuses on conflict—this time conflict between smokers and nonsmokers and between the advisory board and city council regarding the nonsmoking bylaw. (The language reflects a traditional, authoritarian style of leadership.)

Advisory Board Meeting

Executive Secretary: *Does everyone have a copy of the agenda? Do you have a copy of the minutes?*
President: *Can we have a motion on the agenda? On the minutes?*

Business Arising From the Minutes

President: *What about the question of the no-smoking policy?*
Executive Secretary: *Council set a strict no smoking policy for public buildings 3 years ago, and so we moved to make this a smoke-free building effective September 14th. Now council has done an about-face and said we can't enforce it without council's approval.*
President: *Here at the center there has been a campaign from members who smoke, and councilors are getting phone calls. The mayor is livid. He asked that we postpone policy change. I informed him that if council didn't back us on this, I would personally take it as a vote of nonconfidence in me and my board.*

Executive Secretary: *Even if it goes through I expect we are going to have a real problem with smokers. We're going to have to get tough. Same as we are doing with the kids out there in our parking lot next week.*

Past President: *I say we uphold the bylaw and enforce it.*

Social/Education Director: *I'm new and I have a lot to learn. I'm going to be asking lots of questions about things you people already know. Who is our coordinator's supervisor? Who is at the top?*

As social/educational director, Al is a new member on the advisory board, and he has many questions about how business is conducted and who is in charge of what. Now 71 years old, Al retired 6 years ago. He and his wife planned for their retirement and wanted to enjoy life, travel, and volunteer. However, their plans have not been fulfilled as they originally planned. Al explains,

> I'm taking on too much now. I don't have enough time. I get talked into things too easily, and I have trouble saying no. I'm interested in computers, so I was kind of pushed into chairing the computer group. The last thing I got roped into doing was serving on the board. Nobody else would do it. One of the staff called and asked me, and I couldn't say no.

Al thinks that many people avoid becoming involved when they retire because they do not want more responsibilities. Many women who have never been in the public eye are afraid they will "embarrass themselves if they put themselves forward. . . . Two or three female volunteers in the computer classes are very knowledgeable, but they will not teach." The problem is how to build their confidence.

Al developed his confidence to speak in front of a group when he worked as an engineer. The company gave all its employees a public speaking course. On the first day, the instructors randomly selected employees who then had to get up and talk for 2 minutes about anything. Although Al is confident about speaking in a group, he does not enjoy leading one. He finds it frustrating to work with volunteers because he cannot delegate in the same way: "I'm not really a very good manager because I tend to be too soft. When you are dealing with volunteers, you have to be persuasive and that is one of the reasons I am taking the leadership-training course."

Al does not see himself as a leader; he calls himself a "plodder" who follows written guidelines. He sees leaders as visionary people who come up with great ideas all the time, and he is not very happy that he may be expected to become such a visionary. He thinks everyone has good ideas, but they are often too shy to express them.

Leadership in retirement is different, in Al's view, because in business the goal is to make money. He believes that in the business world, you hire employees whom you know are capable, you tell them what to do, and they do it. Conversely, "In retirement, you don't have a choice of the best people for the job; they volunteer. The first question is, 'Are they willing?" The next is, 'Can they do the job?' If they can't, you have to train them," he says.

☐ The Meaning of Life: Beliefs, Values, and Hidden Assumptions

The portrait of Centennial Center reflects a culture of leadership similar to traditional organizational leadership in the business world, with more men than women in formal leadership positions, where men have a stronger voice in the operations of the center. Despite the larger number of women (3:2), their voices are not as clearly heard as were those of women in Carnegie Hall. The women on the board did not participate in the deliberations to the same extent nor with the same enthusiasm as did the men. In contrast to Carnegie Hall, Centennial Center is a place where men have the opportunity to maintain a measure of power and influence enjoyed in their working years. Centennial Center has important lessons to teach us about power and conflict and about the battle of the sexes that appears to rage on into old age. However, a closer examination of what Centennial Center reflects about the nature of retirement, the needs of seniors, leadership, and power is offered first.

The Nature of Retirement

Judging from the variety of activities the center offers to those over 50, retirement is a time to remain both mentally and physically active. The high profile given to athletics suggests that retirement may be the time to develop a level of excellence in such sports as slo-pitch baseball, golf, tennis, and swimming. Seniors can also remain mentally sharp by participating in educational courses such as Introduction to Philosophy, and seniors can even become volunteer teachers in computer classes.

Senior leaders at Centennial Center agree that retirement has generally met all their expectations. As one man said, "Retirement is excellent. It is probably the best—or at least the second best—time of my life. My teenage years were pretty good, too. Fitness is very important: I look after myself and my health has been good" Some seniors are so busy that they do not have enough time for themselves, to go dancing, or to relax. Some are busier now than they ever were when they worked, and few stop to smell the roses in the rose garden.

Many seniors said they joined this center to keep busy and to stay active. Others joined "to make new friends" or "to play a little snooker." Women often joined with their husbands because their husbands retired. Some describe the center as a place to go when they have nothing to do with their time—a place to just hang out. People generally agreed that, as one senior remarked, "the main function is keeping people busy. If someone sits at home and worries, they are better off coming down here and doing some pottery or some embroidery, making something in the workshop or playing table tennis—i.e., exercising body and mind." The center's main function is social: "All the activities are just a vehicle to bring people together."

Increasingly, with the growth and diversity of the membership, retirement is becoming a big business. Certain features of Centennial Center suggest that the organization is a business (e.g., aspects of the environment, the history, the organizational structure, the many references to finances, and the long list of rules for members and conditions under which membership can be terminated). Running such a business requires effective and efficient fiscal and organizational management. In George's view, "Old people don't like to be pushed around, but sometimes it's necessary." People were reluctant, however, to think of their seniors' center as a business, George says, "because I don't think we are here to make money. We are a nonprofit business. If it is a business, we are in the people business . . . the business of living."

One person simply said that the center's function was "to cater to the needs and desires of retired people." The question is, What are the needs and desires that this seniors' center serves?

Needs of Seniors

People have various needs that may influence them to become involved in a seniors' center, and they have certain abilities that might be given expression there. Few people, however, joined the center with the idea of taking on a leadership role, although some found themselves involved. A common reason they gave for assuming more responsibility was that they "couldn't say no" or that they felt "duty bound." A strong element of the Protestant work ethic seems to be operating here, for as one member reflected, "I think everybody *should* do volunteer work. I don't think it's good to just sit and play bingo or play pool all day." Another member added, "Sometimes volunteer work interferes with the square dancing, and my wife and I would rather go dancing!" When asked why anyone would take on a leadership role when they would rather go dancing, everyone agreed it was a good question, but no one could answer it other than to say "Everybody *should* volunteer if they have the time . . . and if they have the time to join, they have the time to volunteer."

Those who chose to volunteer received many rewards. As one woman said, "I always get more out of things than what I put into them. Many people don't know what they might get out of it. They don't believe there is really anything in it for them. If you could convince them of it maybe they would come out." Others talked about a sense of feeling wanted and being appreciated, of accomplishment and achievement. One member remarked that it was a good feeling to know "that what I do to some degree benefits somebody else's life." Being a leader give seniors recognition, a feeling of importance, self-esteem, and energy. George made a direct connection between energy and the challenge that being a leader presented to him:

> One of the advantages of being in a leadership role is to develop whatever it is you are setting out to do, whether it is programs or procedures, in a large organization such as this. We put our brains in gear and we are challenged. We are looking for new problems as well as solutions. I find this particularly energizing to me to be challenged to think. We need to use our brains in spite of getting aged . . . to keep them from going a little grotty later on.

The enthusiasm with which the men debated an issue, such as the smoking or parking problem, was a testament to that energy. And the coordinator concurred: "It is the excitement. I have seen all of you get energized. And I see a wonderful blossoming that has occurred because of your energy. When you get energized, you cause more energetic things to happen around here."

What seemed to prevent people from volunteering at Centennial Center was a pervasive attitude (particularly common to the men) that "I have worked hard all of my life and I don't have to anymore." Many retired people have "had it with the work scene" and believe that they should not be obligated to volunteer, whereas women who have not worked outside the home do not see themselves as leaders and lack confidence in their abilities. Although senior leaders agreed there was an element of power that benefits them, they could not say it was the reason they became involved.

Power

The coordinator is described as a "powerful person," although the designated title of coordinator does not suggest that she has administrative power. She has both administrative skills and power, which she uses judiciously.

Despite formally designated titles of director on the advisory board, members of the board generally believed they had very little power. George was very clear on the matter of the advisory board's power: "Technically we are an advisory board and if anybody wants to listen to our advice that's fine. And if they don't want to take our advice, that's their prerogative." The consensus was that the advisory board plays a major role in initiating change, simply because Alison and her staff try to act in members' best interests. When the coordinator has not been able to initiate change in response to the wishes of the board, she nevertheless represents the interests of seniors to her superiors. For the most part, limitations have been the result of financial constraints. George notes, "Where we spend money that we have earned, we do have the power to make our own decisions. But when the money comes from taxes, we don't. And that is the way it should be." Regarding matters of policy, the coordinator and staff act on the advice of the board, and do the jobs that they believe seniors would not want to do. In that way everyone works together to ensure that policies are carried out and power is shared.

Those who have not had power in their working lives tend to view power as negative, as involving control over others, and as something they do not want. Others, like George, who have exercised considerable power in their professional lives, view it more positively and may fight to maintain a high level of power and influence in retirement. Edward became a volunteer leader in midlife and is enjoying a greater level of power in retirement. He seems frustrated, however, by the fact that he does not have as much power as he would like. (He was surprised to find staff taking on the responsibility of patrolling the parking lot, even though he knows that controversial board decisions, such as those regarding the smoking and parking problems, sometimes threaten the respect and recognition he may want or deserve.)

The conduct of affairs in this center resembles decision making in business, and men are more clearly identified with positions of authority, although power is limited. Both George and Edward's styles of leadership are traditional in their emphasis on power and authority vested in the leader and in the leader's responsibility for setting goals for the group and making decisions according to a democratic process in which the majority rules.

Leadership

Leadership in Centennial Center is similar to traditional leadership in a large business. Being a senior leader in a large organization requires a number of administrative skills, such as taking charge of meetings and making decisions that are not always popular—skills more commonly developed by men than women in the workplace. The difference between leadership in business and in retirement is not always appreciated by everyone. Centennial Center is in the people business, and therefore its focus is on serving members' needs and keeping everyone happy. Along with a traditional view of leadership, there is a general belief that leaders are born—that there are leaders and there are followers. A distinction also is made between leaders and volunteers. Volunteers are not considered to be leaders, nor is their influence in the center fully appreciated. Despite a general belief among members that some people will never be leaders, Alison, the coordinator, insisted that every volunteer was a potential leader. "I think some people are potential leaders and they don't know it. For example, their self-esteem is low. There are some people who have blossomed who never thought they could do it."

Many seniors have the ability, but lack the confidence, and this is especially true for men and women who have not been leaders in the workplace. They need confidence building, encouragement, and support. George claims that the way to begin the process is to

> give people specific tasks. It gets them into some form of group action, and then maybe they will start to talk about their grandchildren or their kids. The reluctant person may be challenged enough to give expression to thoughts that are relevant.

Although many were prepared to admit that good communication skills and sensitivity to people's needs were important qualities for a senior leader, they did not think that leadership in retirement organizations was any different than in the workplace.

In summary, a number of beliefs and assumptions within the culture of Centennial Center serve as barriers to emergent leadership. First, retirement is a time to stay active, mentally and physically, in ways that are personally enjoyable—a time to do what you really want to do. This message conflicts with the Protestant work ethic and a do-gooder mentality that assumes everyone ought to contribute. The coordinator has worked hard to promote retirement as a time for recreation and fun and to dispel the Protestant work ethic that has supplied the "willing horses who do all the work." Many retired people at Centennial Center now choose freely, without guilt, activities that are personally enjoyable, and they no longer feel the obligation to contribute. The center, like many others of its kind, is left with a shortage of volunteers and a need for more creative ways to promote volunteerism and emergent leadership.

Assumptions about traditional leadership act as formidable barriers to the emergence of seniors as leaders in this center: assumptions that the leader must be a visionary who takes charge and makes decisions on behalf of the group, and the view that there are leaders and there are followers and most people will never be leaders. Because the organization is a business, there is a view of leadership as involving the kinds of skills associated with leadership in the workplace, and there is an assumption that men should be in charge.

Assumptions about power act as barriers to emergent leadership also. Women and men who have not been in positions of power in their working lives tend to view power as negative and therefore say that they do not want it or need it. Thus, the people who previously had power and who want to maintain the same level of power in retirement are the ones who assume leadership roles in retirement. Such people often have traditional styles of leadership that perpetuate many of the assumptions about leadership identified in previous chapters, which prevent most older people from becoming more involved, developing their personal potential, and sharing the power and the leadership.

☐ What the Story Reveals About Power and Conflict

A certain amount of conflict is common in any organization, but Centennial Center has more than a healthy share: conflict between the pool players and the board over the smoking bylaw; conflict between the city and the center about the smoking bylaw and who has the power to enforce it; conflict between the students and the seniors over the parking lot; conflict between board and staff regarding who gives out parking tickets to students parking in the seniors' parking lot. And much of the conflict centers around who has authority or power over whom.

People who were asked to speak about power had different views. Women generally said power was something they did not have and did not want. Al said power was something that politicians had, and too much of it was not a good thing. George was a traditional leader who had always had power in his working years and continued to exercise his influence in retirement. Being elected president of a 3000-member seniors' center gave him a degree of power and authority. However, he claimed that seniors really did not have any power in the center. (Is this why some people exerted power to an extreme?) The power the board has is discretionary: board members can really only give advice. (Is this why it is called an advisory board and not a board of directors, so that people would not have the idea they had any real power?)

Empowerment was certainly not a term that applied to George. No one empowered him, although he was visibly energized by an argument. Is this how he empowered himself? His style of leadership was certainly not empowering to others. On the contrary, George's style of interaction excluded all those who avoided conflict and did not enjoy a rousing debate. Because he was a skilled leader and a benevolent dictator, many were content to let George exercise his power as he did. Perhaps the only way to challenge his power is to refuse to engage in the argument. And that is what many people did—certainly most of the women.

Epilogue: How Change Took Place in Centennial Center

Despite the changing nature of retirement and new evidence concerning the desires and capacities of retired people, people (regardless of age) tend to operate from the beliefs and values of a lifetime—the negative stereotypes that limit late-life potential—unless their assumptions are continuously challenged. To challenge these assumptions and change leadership from a traditional approach to a more shared, participatory approach, Centennial Center embarked on a 5-year period of leadership training, and organizational development. The results demonstrate what is possible when skilled and empowering staff work with committed senior leaders to support the kind of intensive training that is required. Collectively, these people are redefining retirement as a time of continuous growth and personal development. They are changing the face of aging and engendering renewed respect for senior citizens as leaders in the community.

In Chapters 7, 8, and 9, details of how transformation took place are translated into practical strategies for professionals and volunteer leaders everywhere who are making the shift from working *for* to working *with* seniors and changing relationships from *powerful* to *empowering* in organizations serving seniors. But first, Chapter 6 presents intimate profiles of three leaders that capture the dynamic interaction between individual motivation and external forces that facilitates the emergence of seniors as leaders.

Three Leaders and How They Found Their Feet

Leadership is growth, and it develops one step at a time. Start people low and slow on the ladder, and support them from rung to rung. Very near the top they will find their own grip.

In this chapter, the focus changes from a broad view of organizational leadership to individual leaders within a particular organizational context and culture. Prototypes are presented of three senior leaders introduced in previous chapters who have transcended the cultural barriers to leadership in their respective organizations and the wider community. Each represents a typical life history with respect to leadership.

To develop a historical perspective, information from personal interviews is used to expand on the portraits of the leaders presented in previous chapters. The individual histories recount experience at various stages of life—education and work history, the third age, and events and opportunities that followed the decision to join a seniors' center that relate to leadership. The chapter concludes with a discussion of relations of power between paid staff and senior volunteers and the components of an empowering relationship. Are leaders born, or are they made? The profiles provide the answers.

☐ Profiles of Leaders

The first profile is of George, the feisty past president of Centennial Center, who represents someone who played an administrative or managerial role during his working years and who transfered these skills to voluntary work during retirement. In this case, the predominant impression of George as leader is one of a strong sense of continuity with what he has been, who he is today, and what he will no doubt continue to be for as long as he is able. Like the professionals in Chetkow-Yanoov's (1986) study of retired professionals in Israel, George has no desire to abdicate his authority or disengage from community life.

The second profile is of Clarisse, the treasurer of Carnegie Hall introduced in Chapter 4, who represents someone who was a leader during working years, who experienced retirement as a critical event not freely chosen, and who subsequently experienced a period of disengagement. With renewed confidence in her abilities, she has reemerged after the death of her only child as a respected leader in her 70s. Her story is one of reconstructing a meaningful and productive role for herself, and the path she took resembles Bengston and Kuyper's social reconstruction model (Payne, 1977).

The third profile is of Florence, the vice-president of Carnegie Hall, a woman not unlike most people who belong to seniors organizations today—women who are widows, mothers, and grandmothers, who never played formal leadership roles in their working lives. Although most do not see themselves as leaders, many have played informal domestic leadership roles, managing home and family. Despite her claim that she was never a leader during her youth or adult years, Florence emerged as a self-confident leader for the first time in her 70th year. Florence's history regarding leadership is one of growth and development of leadership potential that began with retirement from her primary role as wife.

George's Experience: Once a Leader . . .

Trained as a physician in his early years, George studied health care management and enjoyed a long and satisfying career as a hospital administrator during which he "climbed right to the top." In the period just before retirement, he was the administrator of a system of prisons, and he describes that work as challenging and rewarding—so much so that he requested to be allowed to work beyond the age of compulsory retirement. He worked 1 year past the age of 65 while searching for other activities and organizations that might give expression to "my ambition and my drive—I'm insatiable."

When George officially retired, he took on the role of volunteer coordinator for a regional mental hospital, and when he "could not agree with the politics of that organization," he resigned from his formal leadership role and became "just a regular volunteer." During this time, he was also involved in various community organizations, always looking for new opportunities to challenge himself and "climb to the top." One of those organizations was Centennial Center. George's formal education and professional experience prepared him for an administrative role in a large organization delivering service to people, and the position of president of Centennial Center was just what he needed.

George's Life at Centennial Center

George believes that his past experience equipped him well for leadership at Centennial Center, and he describes his most salient leadership qualities as honesty, consistency, and a highly critical nature, which he displays here:

> I'm mad as hell about what's going on with the bus service out here. I see seniors lying on the grass under the tree because there is no place for them to sit and wait for the bus. It's not right that seniors are suffering because the bus company has union problems. Nobody else around here did anything about it. I did! I went right to the top, and I gave the guy who is in charge an earful!

George has a traditional style of leadership and has exercised considerable authority as president. He achieved many of his goals in making the organization run more efficiently and effectively and in giving the office of president greater authority and a higher profile within both the center and the community. In his role as past president, he refers to himself as "somewhat of a has-been" because "the past president doesn't have any power." He considers his responsibilities to be to set the tone at board meetings and assist the newly elected president in running an effective meeting.

During his terms of office, George has become aware of leadership challenges—the serious shortage of people willing to serve in leadership roles and the need for stronger and more effective senior leaders. To improve the leadership, he worked closely with the coordinator to secure funding for a senior leadership development program for members and is exploring ways to encourage the participation of ethnic minorities in programs and activities.

Clarisse's Experience: It Ain't Over 'til It's Over

As a young woman, Clarisse was trained in bookkeeping and clerical skills, ultimately rising to a position of responsibility as a Justice of the Peace. Her professional life spanned 43 years, and she claims she was "still learning right up until retirement." She had considerable power and authority, was highly regarded, and loved her work—so much so that her co-workers often told her she would never be able to retire.

But Clarisse took early retirement to care for her child, who died less than 2 years later. She experienced two major losses in succession—the loss of a demanding and rewarding job and the loss of her only child. Her disengagement was profound and took the form of complete withdrawal from social life. She became reclusive. Clarisse was fortunate to have a close friend who coaxed her out of her self-imposed isolation by convincing her to join a seniors' center. "She saved my life," says Clarisse.

Clarisse's Life at Carnegie Hall

With the increased social and physical activity (i.e., the hiking club) she experienced at Carnegie Hall, Clarisse began to feel better physically and emotionally, and her desire to improve herself slowly returned. "It was very hard at first because I thought my life was over." When the director asked her if she would be interested in working with a group to develop a program designed to build members' confidence and encourage them to participate in group activities, her response was, "This is it, this is learning—this is what I want!" Clarisse enjoyed the opportunity to use the secretarial and bookkeeping skills she had learned as a young woman. When the program was implemented a year later, she enrolled.

The leadership program marked a turning point for her, providing an opportunity to reclaim the skills and talents she had forgotten she had. As confidence in her organizational abilities returned, she became concerned about her failing eyesight. She had been told that she would eventually go blind, and this threatened her ability to participate and eroded her regained confidence. A new doctor gave her hope and performed a surgical technique that restored her vision. Then, when the director asked if she would take on the responsibilities of treasurer of the 2,000-member association, she did not hesitate. With renewed confidence in both her health and her abilities, she felt confident in assuming the role of treasurer.

The treasurer's role made full use of Clarisse's secretarial, bookkeeping, administrative, and teaching skills. The center was becoming a big business, and there was a pressing need to make the system of financial reporting more efficient. Clarisse met the challenge: she devised a more efficient financial system and taught the 34 chairpersons how to implement the system into their respective activity groups. There is a striking similarity between the role Clarisse played as the treasurer of a seniors' center and the one she had played at the height of her professional career when she revised the court system and taught law students how it worked. But there was a difference. In her professional life, Clarisse was very businesslike, efficient, and task oriented. She learned that people come first in seniors' organizations. She adapted her leadership style to become more patient and sensitive to the needs of others.

With encouragement from the president of Carnegie Hall, Clarisse recently joined the board of a mentoring program serving students in a nearby high school who are at risk of dropping out. She derives particular satisfaction from this activity because it places her once again in a teaching capacity with younger people, and, she explains, "leadership to me is more about teaching than anything else."

Florence's Experience: The Time of Her Life

Florence was trained as a nurse; however, like many other women her age, the training was insurance and her real career was marriage and family. Never one to take on a leadership role, Florence said she always hesitated to speak up, even as a child, for fear of making mistakes. Like many married women of her generation, Florence did not think the word *retirement* even applied to her. The premature death of her husband was a highly significant event that released her from her primary working role as homemaker and precipitated her entry into retirement.

Five years passed before Florence made a decision to sell the family home, move to a neighboring community, and begin creating a new social life. She never imagined then that within 3 years she would be having more fun than she had ever had before. And she certainly never dreamed she would be the president of a seniors' center.

Florence's Life at Carnegie Hall

Florence came to Carnegie Hall for the exercise classes, the dancing, the opportunity to meet other single people like herself, and to create a new life. She found that people in the center were friendly, and many were single widows like herself with whom she has "a lot of fun." Like Clarisse, the turning point for Florence was an educational program that presented the opportunity for personal growth.

Florence enrolled in the leadership-training program because she wanted and needed more confidence. Participating in the program gave her a new perspective on herself and her life. During the course of the program, Florence took on two new leadership roles as a result of her newfound confidence. Although she still did not see herself as a leader, she had enough confidence in group situations to take on new challenges. Shortly after the program concluded, Florence was asked by the director if she would consider running for the position of second vice-president of the center. She did not hesitate.

Asked where she learned to be a leader, Florence maintains, "I never was a leader, though I guess I have always been a good listener." She describes herself as "very friendly and easy to get along with. I smile readily and I identify closely with others in the center. I find it easy to listen to people and they seem to find it easy to talk to me. . . and if anyone presents me with a problem or a request, I will see it through to the end."

Florence radiates a quiet calm, warmth, and joy when she reflects on her new sense of accomplishment. "The center fills my life in many ways, and I thoroughly enjoy it, but I do have a life outside." She is also the chair of the housing cooperative in which she lives, and she uses the skills she has learned at Carnegie Hall to chair meetings and delegate responsibilities for managing the cooperative. And she testifies, smiling broadly, "I can do it!" As a result of accepting new challenges and achieving success, her confidence continues to grow.

☐ Are Leaders Really Born or Are They Made?

Was George a born leader? Was Clarisse? Was Florence? There is a widely held assumption that leaders are born. However, qualities and leadership skills are developed throughout life, depending on situations and circumstances. The dynamic interaction between the individual's needs and what the organization offered in the form of personal motivation and sociocultural forces has contributed to the development of each of these three people as leaders in their organizations and in their communities.

Internal Forces: Motivation

What motivated these people to join a particular retirement organization and ultimately assume leadership roles, and what benefits do they derive from their voluntary contributions? All three joined for the social aspects—to be with other people in the third age. This is hardly surprising, since the primary function of a seniors' center is social. However, their individual needs and desires differ.

George

George seemed singular in his need to have an outlet for his personal leadership ambitions, and the role of president of a seniors' center particularly satisfied that need. Furthermore, he recognized that being in a leadership role was critical to his self-esteem. Status and recognition for what he has done and what he is capable of doing helps him to cope with the physical disabilities associated with growing old.

George also admitted that the president of a seniors' center has power, but he adamantly denied a need for power. He maintained that he has been motivated all his life by a desire to help people even when what he achieved was of no personal benefit. He claimed that mental stimulation was particularly critical to his well-being. He began his interview by saying that he was exhausted by caring for a wife who was terminally ill that he did not have the energy to give a proper interview. With each question, his body and his mood changed as his energy slowly returned. He visibly derived energy from the exchange and became more intensely engaged. At the end of the interview, George thanked the interviewer and said how much he had enjoyed the experience and how much better he felt compared with when he arrived. This is an inner power.

George's physical transformation during the interview was dramatic, and this was not an isolated incident. He speaks often about how much he likes a challenge, and enjoys identifying and solving other people's problems. He seems to need a challenge to engage fully in any exchange, and he often appears to provoke an argument to "get the juices flowing." His self-esteem depends on knowing he still has what it takes to run an organization effectively.

Clarisse

Clarisse first joined Carnegie Hall because a friend encouraged her to do so, and she came primarily for the exercise classes and to be with people. After 2 years of isolation, she realized she was missing something; when questioned repeatedly in the interview, she identified that something as the mental stimulation she received in her professional life. She reflected,

I have taken courses all my life because something within me propels me to keep learning. I always had the urge to improve myself. If a job came to where I couldn't learn any more, I'd leave it. I'm in the middle of eight kids, and I have always felt that by improving myself, I could get recognized.

Teaching and learning were what she had always enjoyed and were what she missed most when she retired. "I needed a chance to use my mind, and the more I participated at Carnegie Hall, the more I felt that need being answered."

During the interview, she reviewed her professional life and seemed to gain a greater awareness of the power she had enjoyed. When asked what the word *power* meant to her, Clarisse simply and without hesitation said "energy." Along with the power, she also received considerable respect and recognition. As treasurer of Carnegie Hall, she achieves respect and recognition for what she does, even from people who do not know her. "Everyone around here gets recognition for doing a good job," she says.

Florence

Florence originally joined the center to replace the social role she lost with the death of her husband. After the leadership course, she felt more confident in her abilities than she ever had in the past. "I liked learning about what was happening at the top and I liked being a part of it." She said being a leader just "felt good," and she smiled broadly each time she was asked why she took on so much responsibility when she could be dancing all day and having fun. She also said that she enjoys having some influence and making things happen: "If there are problems, it's nice being part of the solution." She claims that power and status do not appeal to her; she just enjoys the involvement and the feeling of self-confidence and well-being she derives from being part of the action.

Sociocultural Forces: Context

As was apparent from the portraits of leadership in action, Carnegie Hall and Centennial Center are distinctly different organizations. Features of the organizational cultures in which these three people are situated influenced their emergence as leaders in retirement. This section focuses on contextual variables related to the structure and function of each organization, and the relationships among seniors and staff, particularly the relationship between individual members and the professional in charge of each center.

Centennial Center

When George was asked to describe the function of Centennial Center he said, "It is business, social, and recreational. The business is to bring people together and to help them use leisure wisely in whatever way they choose." Recreation for George means mental engagement, challenge, solving problems, and taking charge. Centennial Center was the place for him to exercise his administrative skills and to satisfy his need for challenge and achievement.

In traditional organizational leadership, influence and responsibility for decision making are concentrated at the top. At Centennial Center, much of the power is shared by the coordinator and the president. Although differences of opinion often arise between George and Alison, they are generally resolved amicably. George does not have much contact with staff who carry out the day-to-day operations of the center, although he describes his relationship with "the girls" as good: "I learned to greet them by name, same as the members. If you are interested in people, you take the time." But he adds, "The place is getting too big and it just isn't possible to get to know everybody anymore."

In conducting business, he uses a traditional democratic process to resolve problem issues. This may leave many people unhappy with decisions that are made. For instance, he offers, "Some things come up from time to time, like this bloody smoking thing. The majority didn't want it, and my position was to uphold the bylaw" Sometimes unpopular decisions result in confrontation and conflict. "The group in the pool hall are kind of an ambitious group. The guys are always competing, and that's the nature of the game." When the approach to making decisions is confrontational and competitive, women may be left "out of the game" both by design and by choice, he claims. In many cases, "the boys" in Centennial Center take a competitive approach and maintain a protective attitude toward "the girls," who are sometimes called "dear" and relegated to volunteering in the kitchen and making crafts. Traditional sexist attitudes were often so subtle they passed unnoticed. In one instance of sexist behavior, however, a woman in the pool room became physically violent, attacking one of the men. George knows he has made enemies, because "you just can't please everybody." He views dissatisfaction as a natural consequence of democratic leadership, but does not appear to be aware that his sexist remarks and confrontational style may create unnecessary problems.

Carnegie Hall

In contrast to Centennial Center, Carnegie Hall is a less complex organization with less emphasis on athletic recreation and activity and greater emphasis on providing a safe and comfortable place for seniors to spend their leisure hours. Clarisse views Carnegie Hall as "a place for seniors to feel welcome" as well as "a place to learn." When she first came to Carnegie Hall, she felt vulnerable but found a level of acceptance and comfort, and she eventually had an opportunity to learn. Florence views the function of Carnegie Hall as "a home away from home, providing entertainment for people who don't go out a lot, and particularly single women and men."

Numerous organizational factors (e.g., the smaller size, longer history, fewer members, smaller staff) make it easier for Jo-Ann, as director of Carnegie Hall, to get to know members personally and to nurture their leadership potential. In comparison with Centennial Center, Carnegie Hall is smaller and the membership is less diverse with respect to interests and education. The organizational structure of Carnegie Hall is simple (i.e., all new members receive a copy of the policy and procedures manual, which is brief and easily understood). The community has been supportive of seniors' programs from the beginning. Seniors are more visible and have more voting power. And Carnegie Hall is a safer place for new leaders to test their wings.

The Right Person in the Right Place

Leaders emerge as a process of dynamic interaction between a unique individual and a particular culture. Whether the individual takes on a formal leadership role depends on the right person being in the right place at the right time—with the right kind of support.

In examining Clarisse's and Florence's biographical sketches, one can identify a sequence of timely events and opportunities in combination with personal encouragement and support from others (notably the director) that contributed to their evolution as senior leaders. Clarisse's re-emergence as a leader after retirement proceeded as follows:

1. A friend convinced her to join Carnegie Hall, and accompanied her there.
2. She joined the hiking club and began to feel better physically.
3. The director invited her to join a funding board.
4. Serving on the board provided an opportunity to exercise her secretarial and bookkeeping skills and to learn about the role of confidence in senior participation.
5. Participating in the leadership program increased her self-confidence and administrative skills and presented an opportunity to learn and develop a style of leadership that was more sensitive to the needs of seniors.

6. The director asked her to consider running for treasurer.
7. As a result of serving as treasurer, her confidence in her leadership skills increased.
8. The need to revise the system of financial reporting presented a challenge.
9. Creating a new financial system presented a teaching opportunity, and teaching is consistent with her personal approach to leadership.
10. The invitation to become involved in a mentoring program in the community provided another opportunity to be in a teaching situation and making a contribution to the community.

The progression was from retirement to disengagement to illness to reengagement, to leadership in a seniors' group to educational leadership in the center and, ultimately, to educational leadership in the community.

Similarly, specific contextual influences contributed to Florence's emergence as a leader for the first time in her mid-60s.

1. The director of Carnegie Hall responded to Florence's warm and engaging personality and recognized her listening skills as essential to leadership in seniors' groups.
2. Florence was encouraged by her peers to participate in the leadership program.
3. Participating in the program gave her increased confidence in group situations.
4. During the course of the leadership-training program, she was asked to assume the chair of two activity groups to which she belonged, and she had the confidence to accept these new challenges.
5. Her success as chairperson increased her level of confidence.
6. When the course was over, the director asked her if she would run for the executive board, and she had the confidence to say yes.
7. Her experience as second vice-president has been positive; she says that being a leader "feels good," and she wants more opportunities to play a leadership role.

Leaders both influence and are influenced by organizational culture. The culture of Carnegie Hall is one that encourages and supports the emergence of leaders, and it had a significant influence on the personal development of Clarisse and Florence in their evolution as leaders. In comparison, George did not require training, support, or encouragement to assume a leadership role in the center. He joined Centennial Center as a leader in search of an organization and found a place to challenge his administrative abilities and maintain his self-esteem. However, his authoritarian style of leadership serves to reinforce a traditional view of the leader as someone in charge who takes responsibility for achieving group goals, something few seniors feel qualified to do. Thus, they are quite happy to leave it to George. Furthermore, his confrontational manner is intimidating to many seniors who are less confident of their leadership skills. Thus, the center is left with a shortage of seniors willing to assume leadership roles and a need for a program of leadership development.

As coordinator of Centennial Center, Alison regrets that, because of her increasing administrative responsibilities, she no longer has adequate time to personally motivate, encourage, and support emergent leadership—a common problem for professionals in seniors' organizations that are expanding and providing a greater diversity of services and programs. To address the problem, Alison worked with a board of seniors to offer a program (outlined in the epilogue to Chapter 5) to develop seniors as empowering leaders who can motivate, encourage, and support the development of leadership potential among their peers.

Factors influencing the emergence of seniors as leaders fall into four broad categories:

- Personal motives (needs, desires, aspirations)
- Events and opportunities for engagement and contribution
- Encouragement and support from others
- Personal development and leadership training

When asked, people often found it difficult to identify their motives for assuming a leadership role. Both George and Clarisse articulated their need for mental stimulation. Florence, however, was never able to say specifically what she needed beyond social activity and a bit of fun; she did say she enjoyed learning about how the organization worked and being involved in solving problems. George insisted he was motivated by a desire to help people, and Clarisse said she had always been motivated by a desire to improve herself. On reflection, Clarisse said she was always striving to improve herself as a child because, in a family of eight children, that was how she gained recognition. Although she gets recognition for the work she does at Carnegie Hall, Clarisse cannot say that is why she does it. On the other hand, George readily admitted that he needed status and recognition to counteract the negative aspects of aging.

☐ Relations of Power: Empowerment or Domination?

In Western society, there are many definitions of power, but as Korda (1975) suggested, the dominant view of power is as of having power over others:

All life is a game of power. The object of the game is simple enough: to know what you want and how to get it. The moves of the game, by contrast, are infinite and complex, although they usually involve the manipulation of people and situations to your advantage. (Cited in Kreisberg, 1992, p. 31]

Power is generally perceived to be a scarce resource—covetted, hoarded, and used to one's advantage. In relations of power, there are winners and losers, powerful and powerless, leaders and followers. Relationships of domination are pervasive in work, politics, education, and the family, and they seriously limit one's understanding of power and the possibilities of empowerment.

The traditional concept of organizational leadership extends considerable power and authority to the leader, which may lead to manipulation and control and which can be a problem in seniors' organizations (Cusack, Manley-Casimir, and Thompson, 1992). A style of leadership that is empowering works best in voluntary organizations and most particularly organizations that serve seniors. Kreisberg (1992) claims that "empowerment does not assume control of resisting others, but emerges from work with others who are also deciding, acting, and making a difference" (p. xi). He defines empowerment as a personal transformation out of silence and submission that is characterized by the development of an "authentic voice." He suggests that to be empowered is to have "the ability to make a difference, to participate in decision-making and to take action for change" (p. xi).

Kreisberg describes personal and political relationships within which power is shared as an expanding resource in which the experience of power elicits further expressions of power from others. Strength is expressed in openness to the voices of others and to change, as well as in innovation and trust in the growth that comes as people work together. "Power with" is power among equals. It is the type of power required for people to become active participants in shaping the social and economic structures that affect their lives. It is this kind of "power with" that concerns those who work to empower seniors in a variety of contexts across North America, and it is inherent in the concept of shared servant leadership proposed in Chapter 2.

☐ Relations of Power Between Seniors and Professionals

Fundamental to the relationship between seniors and professionals is the professional's attitude toward seniors—his or her ability to recognize each human being for their uniqueness and to communicate confidence in their abilities. For both Alison and Jo-Ann, recognizing individual need and leadership potential are a priority. However, with the increasing demands placed on staff in many seniors' organizations, few professionals have the time or the expertise to cultivate individual leadership potential in the way that Jo-Ann nurtured the personal potential of Clarisse and Florence. Alison specifically identified the need for leadership training in Centennial Center as a way of developing new leaders.

Educational programs develop both confidence in the skills gained over a lifetime and new skills for participating effectively in groups. Whereas Clarisse lost her confidence and just needed to reclaim skills she already had, Florence developed confidence, an awareness that her caregiving and listening skills were valued, and new leadership skills. Without both education and personal support, it is unlikely that either Clarisse or Florence would be recognized as the self-confident senior leaders they are today. (As an addendum, 6 months after the completion of this study, Clarisse published a seniors' column in the local newspaper and Florence was elected president of Carnegie Hall).

One of the purposes of leadership training for retirees is to educate more traditional leaders, such as George, about how to share the power and the responsibilities with others and how to encourage and support the contributions of their less confident peers. In many cases, the challenge is not just to convince the more traditional leaders that leadership in retirement is different but to convince them that they can benefit from a training program.

These profiles provide evidence that the third age is neither a time to disengage from community life nor a time to continue to share the workload out of a sense of duty and "because somebody has to do it." Rather, it is a time for personal development, achievement, and self-fulfillment. These seniors expressed a need to contribute and volunteering affords them that opportunity. If they engage in volunteer roles that are personally fulfilling and they receive adequate recognition for the work they do, people will continue to contribute in ways that are mutually beneficial to individuals and organizations for as long as they live, just as George, Clarisse, Florence, and thousands of others are doing.

PART

III

THE PRACTICE OF
LEADERSHIP

Part III provides practical instructions to all who believe that older people have unique and vital contributions to make, who see problems as challenges and age as opportunity. Chapter 7 describes the shift from power to empowerment and how to be a catalyst. Chapter 8 focuses on personal leadership style and how to become an empowering leader. And Chapter 9 returns to the basics of leadership training, but with an appreciation for the kind of education and training that transforms individuals, groups, and communities in extraordinary ways. This frees older people from negative images of old age that too often serve as self-fulfilling prophecies, motivating and inspiring them to achieve their full potential as persons and to leave a rich legacy that benefits all those who follow them.

Creating a Culture of Leadership

Good leadership consists of motivating people to their highest levels by offering them opportunities, not obligations. . . . Life is an opportunity and not an obligation.

—Heider, 1988, p. 135

This chapter takes a deeper look at the needs and desires of seniors and what they need to help them climb to the top of a new mountain. The changing nature of retirement, the changing capacities and needs of seniors, the changing mandates, the conflicts over competing priorities—all the uncertainty and ambivalence represent the chemistry of change. This chemistry can be used as a catalyst to create change, to move an organization toward a more equitable and inclusive sharing of power, and to create empowering relations between staff and members. Implementing a program of leadership development requires more than just a needs assessment and a leadership-training program. It means challenging old assumptions and changing negative assumptions to positive ones. It means understanding issues of power and dealing with conflict. It means offering the kind of education that empowers. This chapter concludes with an appreciation for the role of education and research in the emergence of effective leadership.

139

☐ Climbing to the Top

Many people find it difficult to identify their needs—particularly to identify why they might take on a leadership role. When senior leaders were asked, "Why would anyone want to take on more responsibilities in retirement when they could spend the time dancing and having fun?," the response was usually, "Good question!" No one had an answer that was insightful or satisfying. Many said they liked to help others or they felt a sense of obligation, but no one said they needed or wanted power.

Many people, like Florence (the vice-president of Carnegie Hall profiled in Chapter 6), have never before experienced the sense of power that a leadership role affords them, and they say they neither need it nor want it. Yet the more they speak their own mind, the more influence and power they have, the better they feel. People generally want to feel good, but power is not commonly associated with energy and feeling good. For people like George (the past president of Centennial Center profiled in Chapter 6) who have always had power, it is something they need. Whether they admit it or not, power is critical to their self-image and self-esteem.

Maslow's hierarchy helps to explain needs and desires of seniors that might motivate them to assume a leadership role. The reasons people give for joining a seniors' center are varied and may be as specific as "because I wanted to play pool when it rains and I can't go golfing." But that's not the *real* reason they joined. The main reason for joining and the primary function of a seniors' center is social. Joining a seniors' center, or any other group, generally satisfies Maslow's third level of need for belonging. After people have met their need for acceptance and belonging, they may assume a volunteer role, that is, they feel a desire to contribute. It is at the fourth level of Maslow's hierarchy that a need begins to be associated with a desire or expression of intentionality—the ego's need for respect, self-esteem, recognition.

Clarisse, the treasurer of Carnegie Hall who reemerged as a leader after a period of disengagement, recognized that she always strived to improve herself as a child because that was how she gained recognition. Although she is recognized for the work she does at Carnegie Hall, she claims that is not why she does it. Seniors have difficulty admitting they need recognition, perhaps because of the prevailing assumption that retirement is a time to leave the work and achievement behind, a time for seniors to withdraw from public life. So why would they need to be recognized? Many seniors assume new leadership roles after retirement and continue to develop their leadership potential provided they receive adequate recognition. One senior leader said, "If you don't get recognized, you say to hell with it!"

For many people, *status* was an aggravating word associated with power. Considerable ambivalence surrounded the concept of power. Words that came to mind included *authority, fear, opportunity, knowledge, ability, energy, action, coercion,* and *security.* One woman claimed that seniors did not think highly of people who took on leadership roles for the status and recognition. Yet George readily admitted he needed both status and recognition to counteract the negative aspects of aging. Status and power seem to have negative connotations for those not accustomed to having them and positive value for those who (like George and Clarisse) have enjoyed a measure of them throughout their lives. However, recognition was something everyone agreed was essential. Significantly, one senior leader who insisted that seniors do not need recognition wanted to know whether her name would appear as a contributor to a training manual. Another said, "From the cradle to the grave, isn't our task to be recognized? Who wants to pass through life with no one knowing you were here?"

Seniors have needs much the same as people of any age, although losses commonly associated with age, including the event of retirement, put them at risk and erode their confidence and self-esteem. Many seniors need to develop more confidence in their abilities before they are willing to assume responsible roles. After a level of self-confidence is achieved, many express the need for a sophisticated challenge and a desire to contribute their personal skills and talents to the betterment of the organization. After people gain the recognition they need, they will continue to develop their potential and make significant contributions in the groups to which they belong. With a sense of belonging (level 3) and adequate respect and recognition (level 4), seniors are motivated to develop their full potential as people, climbing to the top of Maslow's hierarchy in later life.

The profiles of senior leaders provide compelling evidence that the third age is a time of continuous personal development and self-fulfillment for many older adults. And if there are many seniors who have the potential to contribute to community life in ways that give full expression to their unique life experience, then a clear mandate for seniors' organizations is that they create the kinds of organizational cultures in which such development and expression becomes possible.

☐ A New Mandate for Seniors' Groups and Organizations

Although the primary role of a seniors' center is to provide socialization, an increasingly diverse array of services is offered. Most seniors' organizations exist to provide a service to seniors. The service-providing organizational model sees the role of the leader as providing service to the client.

Many people leading seniors' groups interpret this as making decisions *for* older people, when what seniors really need is an opportunity to develop their personal potential and contribute their particular skills and talents to the betterment of the group. In other words, promoting the personal development of individuals and their full participation in community life is more important than achieving organizational goals. Neither center, however, explicitly stated personal growth or leadership development as part of the center's policy.

An explicit function of all organizations that serve seniors ought to be the personal and leadership development of members, and that means a new approach to leadership is required. The professional leader's primary role should be to create a culture of leadership in which the full participation of all persons is promoted, encouraged, and recognized. Such a mandate is premised on a more optimistic and increasingly more tenable view of late life potential and a view of the third age or retirement phase as a time to create a meaningful and productive role.

The creation of a culture of leadership begins with an appreciation for the nature of retirement and the fundamental needs of the retired people whom the organization is designed to serve. What is characteristic of retirement and retired people? Retirement marks the end of a professional career or working life for most men; for many women, it means the end of a demanding family role (i.e., that of wife or mother). For some it is experienced as a long-awaited release from tiring and often unfulfilling work, an opportunity to relax, travel, play golf, read, or rediscover a forgotten or undeveloped talent. As a rite of passage, it is unique because it is incomplete (Jarvis, 1989). Unlike other rituals in life (e.g., marriage or graduation), retirement marks a transition "out of," with no sense of what is beyond, what to expect, or how to prepare for it. Regardless of whether retirement is experienced as a welcome or a traumatic event, it involves the loss of a productive role. Bennis (1990) claims that "more than 90% of the employed population work in formal organizations. Status, position, a sense of competence and accomplishment are all achieved in our culture through belonging to these institutions." (p. 135).

Older people are distinguished by their diversity of lifestyles, health, and income, but most importantly by the knowledge and skills developed over a lifetime of personal, practical, and professional experience in the workplace, the family, and the community. Seniors are unique in ways that 5-year-olds and 20-year-olds are not. As a result of retirement and the loss of a designated role in society, many experience the sense that they are not recognized and valued as persons. Everyone needs to feel good and be recognized as a person of worth. Regardless of whether retirement is freely chosen, it is a time for every individual to establish a particular role that provides a sense of meaning and purpose.

What humans need to survive and what they need to flourish are different matters. The human capacity for learning and growth continues well into later life, provided opportunities and incentives are available (Moody, 1988). However, although social policy typically offers seniors help with basic needs, it offers little opportunity to address higher level needs. As Butler (1975) suggests, people tend to settle for mere survival when so much more is possible:

> Man thinks of himself as wise and distinguished from other animals by his capacities for forethought, language, and symbolic thinking, and for the transmission of culture. And yet we have failed to maintain conditions which bring those capacities to their fulfillment. Those qualities which are especially associated with middle and later life—experience, accumulated skills, knowledge, judgment, wisdom, and perspective—are discarded just when they are coming to fruition in human beings. (p. 64)

If the potential for continuous personal development throughout the life span is accepted, the role of the leader, whether a professional or senior volunteer leader, should be as Bennis (1990) claims—"to create not only a climate of ethical probity but a climate that encourages people to learn and grow, prizes their contributions, and cherishes their independence and autonomy" (p. 146). The task is to create the environment and opportunity through which each member can satisfy individual needs for continued growth and expression of personal skills, talents, and knowledge. For many seniors, part of that development involves assuming formal leadership roles, roles that will be much different from the authoritarian model to which many have been accustomed.

☐ The Chemistry of Change

The portraits of the two seniors' centers reveal assumptions about the needs of seniors, about the nature of retirement, and leadership and power that serve as barriers to emergent leadership. Stereotypes common in society about the nature of retirement, the needs of seniors, power, and leadership act as formidable barriers to the emergence of seniors as leaders. The prevalence of these assumptions helps to explain why so many seniors are reluctant to assume leadership roles.

In Carnegie Hall, a timely sequence of opportunities, events, and interactions served to overcome certain barriers and facilitate the emergence of seniors as leaders. The empowering style of the director was a key to the emergence of leaders. Leadership-training courses offered at Carnegie Hall during recent years have promoted a concept of shared-servant leadership, an approach that differs from the traditional one and is considered to be more effective in seniors' groups.

The study of the culture of Centennial Center was undertaken after recognition of the need for more able and willing senior leaders and before the implementation of a leadership-training program. Consequently, it was not surprising to find a more traditional approach to leadership at Centennial Center.

In retirement groups, a traditional authoritarian style of leadership is a particular problem because many retired people have lost a certain status associated with the workplace, and they may be particularly vulnerable to loss of confidence and self-esteem. The leader who operates from a position of authority and control, even if coercing people for what he or she sincerely believes to be in their best interests, may have an insidiously harmful effect on individual autonomy. Not only do people who take power away from others rob group members of energy and vitality during meetings, they may also have a detrimental effect on the physical and emotional health of group participants.

In many ways, George fits the picture of the benevolent dictator. He saw himself as someone dedicated to serving and helping other people, yet he said, "Seniors don't like to be pushed around, but sometimes it's necessary." Regardless of whether the leader considers himself or herself to be working in the best interests of those he or she is leading, failure to respect their rights and freedoms often diminishes them and may create further dependency. Although the structure of Centennial Center suggests that power is shared between the coordinator and the board, narrative suggests that power is not shared. Rather, the men in the center jockeyed for power. Certainly power was not equitably shared by members of the board, nor was it shared with most of the women, who did not seem to have a voice in the center's affairs.

☐ Sharing the Power

People are motivated by a need to maintain the same margin of power and control as they enjoyed in earlier years. Some support that view, yet claim that power is not something they need. Others are able to identify the power they experienced in their professional lives and to feel a renewed sense of energy from that power. For others, power has negative connotations. Is it having power that makes people feel good? Or is it the confidence and self-esteem derived from exercising power?

The question is, To what extent does a strong traditional leadership style deter less confident and less-experienced seniors from becoming more involved and taking on a leadership role? The traditional approach to leadership often fails to give voice to those who are less confident in their leadership abilities (notably women).

People who have not had power in their adult lives, whether men or women, may not feel the need for power. Yet when seniors experience a sense of power as a result of their work, it often gives them a feeling of exuberance and well-being. If people have had power and then lost it prematurely, the need to have it again may be excessive. This need may then become unhealthy, creating an insatiable need for power and an inability to feel the satisfaction, exuberance, or well-being that accompanies recognition and achievement. Such is the case with many traditional leaders, who may derive little satisfaction from their insatiable drive for power while denying others the opportunity for meaningful involvement and contribution. If that power is not legitimate (e.g., when the board is an advisory board that can be overruled), the traditional leader who wants and needs a degree of power may justifiably feel frustrated and disempowered.

Clearly, seniors want to remain independent, to have a measure of power and control over their lives, and to experience a measure of influence in the groups and organizations to which they belong. Negative connotations of power, lack of confidence in one's abilities, and a belief in one's powerlessness in groups serve as barriers to emergent leadership. The assumption tends to be that there are those who have power over others and those who do not. And because traditional leadership is a lonely enterprise that does not facilitate connections between people, it seems reasonable to expect that few people who join a seniors' organization to fill a need for belonging and connectedness with a community of peers will want to assume a leadership role. Yet the central mandate of social services is to empower seniors—that is, to give them power over their own lives. The concept of empowerment as taking control of oneself ignores the aspect of connecting with people. Such power seldom occurs in isolation.

☐ Creating Empowering Relationships

One cannot escape the notion of power as domination , which may lead to manipulation and control that is harmful to group members. Power, however, need not be exclusionary. Kreisberg (1992) explores the concept of power in a way that suggests how one can create relations of power between people that are empowering for everyone:

> Empowerment is the ability to make a difference, to participate in decision-making and to take action for change. Empowerment does not assume control of resisting others, but emerges from work with others who are also deciding, acting, and making a difference. (p. xi)

Kreisberg describes personal and political relationships within which power is shared as an expanding resource, in which the experience of power elicits further expressions of power from others. Strength is expressed in openness to the voices of others, to change, to innovation, and to trust in the growth that comes as people work together. *Power with* is power among equals. It is the type of power required for people to become active participants in shaping the social and economic structures that affect their lives.

Sharing power involves changing the orientation from the traditional one of *power over* to an orientation of power with. The president and the coordinator or director are the two most powerful people in seniors' organizations, and their relationship often provides the model and sets the tone for staff and seniors. The relationship between Jo-Ann and Margaret, the key leaders in Carnegie Hall, is an empowering one: Jo-Ann's sensitivity to members, her encouragment and support of their contributions, counteracts Margaret's traditional authoritarian style that tends to shut people down, especially the men. On the other hand, the relationship between George and Alison can be characterized as a powerful one based on equality, shared responsibility, trust, and respect for the other's perspective. The difference is one of relative emphasis on the needs of the individual versus the goals of the organization. An empowering relationship has the following qualities: openness, trust, support, care, and concern for others' needs and perspectives and face-to-face communication. An empowering relationship is more than just an effective relationship that gets the job done. The subtle difference lies in the relative emphasis placed on the care and concern for the other person (their perspective and needs) and the need to complete the task. In an empowering relationship, the focus is on the people, and the quality of the relationship is less instrumental and more personal: the work gets done but with a more enjoyable and satisfying result. It begins with a deep understanding of the other person—their needs, goals, and aspirations. As one board member said, "Sharing a deep understanding is empowering in itself." One can then empower the other person by providing whatever they need to enable them to develop their full potential as leader.

☐ Implementing a Program of Leadership Development

To assist seniors in developing meaningful roles for themselves in the organizations to which they belong, requires educational opportunities that help them to recognize and enhance existing skills and, in many cases, to develop new ones. Education can play an important role in developing not only leadership skills but also the level of self-confidence and self-esteem needed to participate fully in community life. Furthermore, the training people must challenge them to believe in their leadership potential, to communicate more confidently, to approach leadership in a new way with an emphasis on people rather than the task, and to appreciate the needs and the potential of all seniors to share in the leadership and the power.

Conducting a Needs Assessment

This chapter has explored what seniors want and need. Why would anyone want to conduct a needs assessment? Because it offers an opportunity for leaders to listen in a new way to what seniors really need and want. It presents an opportunity to do the following:

- Begin an authentic dialogue based on equality and respect
- Learn more about their skills, experience, and background knowledge
- Look more closely at the organization, what people do, what they are trained to do, and what will give them confidence in their abilities and skills

If possible, a trained researcher or consultant who has the necessary background in organizational leadership and sensitivity to seniors issues should be engaged, one who can involve every member of the organization in the discussions and explorations to achieve a common understanding and commitment. Leadership training cannot be considered outside of the context in which it is taking place. When a program is designed that reflects a deep understanding of the culture, the needed training can then be offered that will increase the understanding of the leader-student, enhance his or her leadership skills, and improve the quality of leadership. To be highly successful, people require more than just a training program. They need and deserve the kind of expert training and education that empowers people.

More Than Just a Training Program

What kind of education empowers seniors? The teacher-facilitator who intends to empower others does not give up authority and responsibility but actively works to transfer the responsibility for learning to the students. Education that empowers involves a shift from power as domination to power as creative energy. A view of power as creative energy requires that strategies be developed to counteract unequal power relationships and to move the dynamics toward equality of power.

Empowering students involves a continuous process of dialogue and negotiation between facilitator and learner with the emphasis on balancing individual and group training needs. Confidence in one's leadership skills and abilities does not occur as a result of injecting of topics x, y, and z into the discussion; rather, it develops through continuous discussion, practice, feedback, reflection, and renegotiation focusing on topics that relate to the tasks involved in leadership. The essence of empowerment pedagogy is classroom discussion, and the facilitator must be highly skilled and able to incorporate strategies for facilitating new learning and critical thinking.

Seniors who participated in a leadership training program clearly understood that a skilled facilitator was essential to any educational program. They said the teacher-facilitator must be one who does the following:

- Understands that the participants are the experts and the teacher is the guide
- Listens well and has patience and good control of the more vocal members of a group
- Takes a participatory approach, sets ground rules, deals with feelings, and ensures that everyone can see and hear
- Ensures that everyone has an opportunity to engage in discussion, realizing that the shy and quiet ones may need extra encouragement
- Obtains group feedback and adapts each session accordingly
- Respects the contribution seniors have to give and the wisdom they have accumulated over the years
- Challenges and stimulates thinking to change attitudes that block new insights
- Believes in each person's potential and the possibility for new growth
- Uses humor effectively
- Never underestimates what seniors have to offer: there is no limit to what they know and what they can do, because age is just a number.

The success of any leadership-training program may rest on whether someone with the essential skills can be engaged to facilitate the training. And as part of the training program, the facilitator must help people to understand and deal with issues of power and conflict.

Addressing Issues of Power and Dealing With Conflict

A number of issues, often expressed as frustrations or problems, are "disempowering" for seniors. If they are not addressed, they often lead to disappointment, loss of motivation for seniors and staff, and withdrawal from activities and contributions that could be enjoyable and life enhancing. They sometimes lead to more serious conflicts, affecting the health of individuals and the entire organization. As one senior leader suggested, "I think some people have to make themselves sick before they are able to give up their control."

These tales suggest differences between men and women in their orientation to leadership and power. When asked to speak about power, women generally said power was something they did not have and did not want. To the contrary, George often provoked confrontation and conflict because it kept his juices flowing. Empowerment was not a term that applied to George: no one empowered him and his style of leadership was not empowering—rather, it excluded those who did not enjoy debate and conflict. Men and women generally have different views of power, reflected in Kreisberg's definition of "power with" and "power over."

Power from a traditional, power over, perspective includes words like *control, domination,* and *authority*. These words reflect the "language of domination" and are commonly associated with traditional leadership. However, relations of power in which power is shared are associated with words such as *strength, energy,* and *vitality*—that is, the language of empowering leadership or what is called the "language of possibility".

In both centers, there were differences in perceptions of power according to gender. Most women expressed negative attitudes toward power and did not feel they wanted it. When they were encouraged to view power as something that they may want to have, it was described as a "gentle power of influence". In contrast, the men generally viewed power as authority and responsibility. Men tended to have power-over orientations to power and to use the language of domination in speaking about power, whereas women tended to speak of power using the language of possibility.

There are two aspects of power: (1) to give legitimate authority or responsibility, and (2) to enable people to assume that authority or responsibility. The aspect of empowerment that men tended to focus on was creating legitimate opportunities for people to exercise their skills—that is, the first part of the definition. Some leaders have a notion of power and empowerment that reflects a typically male perspective: empowering people means "throwing them the ball and letting them run with it." The assumption is that seniors already have the tools, all they need is the invitation (and men typically have experience, knowledge and skills from leadership roles in the workplace). For both senior women and female staff, empowerment more often included all the "touchy-feely" things—encouragement, support, confidence building, in addition to providing knowledge and leadership training.

Narratives in Chapters 4 to 6 support gender differences in orientations to power and also suggest that how one empowers men may be different from how one empowers women. Are men from Mars and women from Venus, as Gray (1992) concluded? In other words, are women and men essentially different? There are clear exceptions to the rule: women such as Margaret, who tend to operate from a traditional orientation, and men like Edward, the new president of Centennial Center, who have not been leaders in their earlier years and have a more nurturing and empowering orientation toward leadership.

Arguments against making distinctions on the basis of gender (i.e., the essentialist position) go beyond the exception to every rule. Attributing differences to gender leads to gender stereotyping, and assumptions of difference often lead to unintended consequences that perpetuate the battle between the sexes. In reality, it is not the essential gender difference, but rather life experience and professional training that determine a person's style of leadership in retirement. Women who have been in traditional leadership roles in business typically have the same perspective as men with the same professional background, and they often have the same style of leadership. Furthermore, although notions of "power with" are drawn from the feminist movement, assuming a feminist perspective invariably excludes men. (Margaret was a strong traditional leader and a feminist whose negative attitudes toward men discouraged them from participating.)

A better distinction between power-with and power-over orientations can be made on the basis of language rather than gender—better because it is more useful. George, for example, dedicated his life, as a physician and later as a leader in Centennial Center, to serving other people. It was not his focus on the task at the expense of the individual that was so harmful, but his aggressive, sexist language. Using a cultural perspective and an approach to research grounded in critical ethnography, one can identify traditional, repressive cultures through the dominant discourse and exclusive language associated with a traditional orientation and can begin to create a new language that is more inclusive, a language of possibility that truly empowers people.

Transforming the organizational culture from a power-over to a power-with approach requires more than organizational effectiveness and leadership training. The term *organizational effectiveness* connotes efficiency and effectiveness in achieving a goal or end result—a concept associated with traditional leadership in which the goals of the organization are paramount and supersede the needs of all individuals. Organizational transformation begins with a deeper understanding of the needs, desires, beliefs, and values of the membership. Changes that follow may encompass changing attitudes and beliefs, organizational mandates and structures, and the quality of working relationships. It certainly includes changing the language people use from one of domination to one of possibility. People who have the freedom to choose, because they are retired, are more likely to assume leadership roles in groups and organizations if they are invited, encouraged, supported, inspired, and recognized rather than appointed, delegated, or seconded.

Some examples of how to change the language are provided in the lists below.

Traditional Language	Language of Possibility
Power over	**Power with**
board of directors	advisory committee
director	coordinator
president	chair
conflict	concern
delegate	ask/invite
lead	serve
the task comes first	the people come first
leaders and followers	group of leaders
speaking	listening
effective leadership	empowering leadership
energy depleted	energy charged
resistance to change	openness to change
criticism	feedback

☐ The Role of Education in the Emergence of Seniors as Leaders

Education is the key to developing leadership. The quality of the learning experiences offered is as critical as the support and encouragement from empowering leaders. This is how one leader in Carnegie Hall found her niche in life at the age of 76:

> I am a self-confident person today, but I was not always that way. Shyness has been a drawback throughout my life. My story covers a period of 12 years and it begins with the death of my husband. Within the year, I took early retirement from a very busy job. I soon felt I needed more fulfilling activities to replace two major losses—of spouse and job. Because we had moved around so much, I also felt the need for a sense of security. In other words, I had to find my niche.
>
> I was persuaded by a friend to join the seniors' center. My friend was in the exercise class, and because I needed her support in this new venture, I

joined that class, too. I soon warmed to the camaraderie and discovered the enjoyment of participation in a group. I also benefited from the exercise.

My first in-class learning experience was a health promotion program. I discovered how much fun it could be learning with my peers who wanted to live healthier lives and felt the same sense of empowerment. The facilitator was so inspiring that I took the follow-up course. To this day, I still benefit from the knowledge I gained.

When I heard that the Red Cross was giving a senior volunteer instructor course for their Fun & Fitness Program, I signed up for it. Where that bit of bravado came from, I'll never know. I enjoyed the course, but the very thought of standing up in front of a class that looked to me for guidance made me nervous. That first day the exercises seemed more complicated than usual and I made a few blunders—like asking people to put their elbows on their shoulders. However, I learned in those early weeks to laugh at myself, and as I relaxed, so did the class. That's when the fitness class really became fun.

A year later, a peer counseling course was advertised at the center. It caught my interest. During that training program, I learned more about myself than I could have ever imagined. At the end of the first year, the senior peer counselors learned that the program was now ours to manage and administer—to keep client records, to liaise with other agencies, to raise funds, and to make presentations. It was then that our center offered a leadership course facilitated by two adult educators. In that course, I gained self-confidence and self-esteem, and learned how to work more effectively in committees.

The follow-up program was a public speaking course especially for seniors. I wanted more confidence. After the first two sessions, I decided that I had bitten off more than I could chew and was becoming a nervous wreck. But the facilitator understood and, edged me past my comfort zone. I plodded on. The applause for my speech on the last day of the class made it all worthwhile.

When I embarked on my lifelong learning program, I never anticipated the changes it would make to my life. As I look back, I am aware of how I am continually rising to new challenges and surviving. More than surviving, I have achieved a level of competence and self-confidence that I never dreamed was possible. Today, I cofacilitate a discussion group, a program that helps seniors who lack social skills (for whatever reason) to feel comfortable conversing and reminiscing with their peers. In my role as facilitator, I use all of my newly acquired skills to enrich the lives of others. I want to go on learning and to inspire other interested seniors to keep their minds active. In our rapidly changing world, we should all be aware of the technological changes, even if we don't understand them. We have to stay positive and keep a sense of humor.

Education is the key that has opened many doors for me and other seniors at our center. We have benefited from skilled adult educators who have shared their expert knowledge in a safe, comfortable environment, always stimulating our minds and creating in us the wanting to know more. With their expert instruction and inspiration, and the guidance and support of the director and staff, I have truly found my niche in life.

A primary role for older adult education is to develop a critical cultural awareness among the growing populations of people aged 50 and over—that is, to help people to understand how organizational structures and cultures influence the quality of their lives and to recognize when their creativity, motivation, initiative, and skills are being eroded. The education of older adults is not simply an extension of adult education to a new group of people, it is a different kind of education. It is the kind of education that addresses the issue of older people's political and social emancipation and contributes to the transformation of people and society.

Aronowitz and Giroux (1991) refer to contested public spheres' as places that have the potential to contribute to social transformation. They suggest that schools be such places. Seniors' centers should also be such places. And every seniors' group and organization has the potential to contribute to such personal and social transformation.

Society's negative attitudes toward older people, reflected in the culture of these seniors' centers—attitudes that seriously limit late-life potential—are ones that future generations will inherit. It is essential that educational leaders work with today's seniors and the professionals who serve them to create opportunities for enrichment and engagement —a new old age of meaning and possibility—that will be their legacy. In Chapter 8, the focus is on leadership style and how to become a more effective and empowering leader.

CHAPTER

8

Transforming Leadership

> Leaders are made, they are not born; and they are made just like anything else has ever been made in this country—by hard work. And that's the price we all have to pay to achieve that goal, or any goal.
>
> —Vince Lombardi

There are many ideas about what and who is a leader. Throughout history different kinds of leadership have been prevalent as the typical behaviors of leaders and group members have shifted, depending on the expectations that each held of the other. Their roles have always been interdependent and influenced by the situation in which they are operating and the tasks involved. The process of leadership involves two major players—the leader and the group members; there can never be one without the other. Leaders have qualities, skills, and personalities, and so do members. Leaders have expectations, past experience, and vision, and so do members. Both are affected by the situation, the task, and the times. Typically, the various approaches to understanding leadership focus on (1) qualities and traits of a good leader, (2) skills associated with being a leader, (3) importance of the situation, and (4) different styles of leadership. These four aspects offer a deeper understanding of how effective leadership functions in retirement.

One common approach to understanding leadership is to focus on the qualities associated with being an effective leader. Words such *traits, characteristics, attributes, attitudes, values,* and *abilities* are also used to describe qualities. The problem with using qualities to determine whether one has what it takes to be a leader is that qualities do not work on their own. The qualities attributed to leadership are not all that make leaders great. Before reading through the list of qualities think about the leadership qualities you may possess.

☐ Leadership Qualities

How many of these qualities do you have? Do you know of a leader who has most of these qualities? Some of them? This list is included to illustrate and emphasize how difficult it is to use qualities alone as a means of defining an effective leader.

integrity	empathy	cooperative
compassion	caring	gracious
intelligent	organizational skill	inspirational
enthusiasm	respectful	imaginative
patience	wise	approachable
courage	conscientious	emotionally stable
aware	committed	energetic
self-confidence	judgment	trustworthy
perceptive	trusting	risk-taker
optimistic	resilient	assertive
ambitious	stamina	cheerful
insightful	charismatic	dedicated
tenacious	honest	giving
advocate	thoughtful	helpful
stress resistance	perseverance	loving
sincere	creative	courteous
humanitarian	strong	humorous
tolerant	desire to serve others	relaxed
forthright	sensitive	thoughtful
resourceful	cheerful	objective
friendly	dependable	pleasant
diplomatic	interest in people	initiative
good voice	broadminded	
punctual	fair	
flexible	understanding	
dynamic	encouraging	

☐ Leadership Skills

Similarly, if you look at the following list of skills, you may conclude that some leaders have some of these skills, but seldom does one person possess them all. How many do you have? How do you know you have these skills? How do you measure them? Which ones do you think others see in you?

solve problems	help others use their strengths
develop a team spirit	give wise counsel
clarify goals	express ideas clearly
communicate	deal with disruptive people
listen	motivate others
inspire	evaluate
make people feel welcome	generate enthusiasm
chair a meeting	draw on personal knowledge
delegate responsibilities	plan and follow through
get things done	take charge when necessary
build confidence	share power and control
facilitate a discussion	hold interest
get the best out of people	make others feel needed
understand the needs of others	encourage and support

The good thing about skills is that they can be learned, and they can always be developed and improved.

> Being the leader doesn't make you one, because leaders don't automatically get the respect and acceptance of their group members; so in order to earn the leadership of their group and have a positive influence on the group members, leaders must learn some specific skills and methods.
>
> —Thomas Gordon

☐ Leadership Styles

Ask yourself the following questions:

What is your style?
What words would you use to describe it?
What words would other people use to describe your style?
What is working with your style? How do you know?
What is not working with your style? How do you know?
How will you change it?

How do you share the leadership?

Do volunteers in your organization work for you or do they work with you?

Are the volunteer seniors in your organization empowered?

Are you a listener rather than a talker?

Do you act from a genuine concern for others?

Do you challenge and develop leadership potential in others?

Do you stimulate and inspire the quality of excellence?

There are a variety of styles of leadership, each appropriate in certain situations but not in others. The *laissez-faire style* in which anything goes rarely works well, except perhaps on an extended vacation. The *democratic style* in which the majority rules works for some groups but not for others and only some of the time. The take charge, *autocratic or authoritarian style* of leadership is appropriate in emergencies or when there is no time to make a group decision (e.g., in case of fire). *Shared leadership* occurs when responsibility for leadership is shared among the members. Some people in retirement want to take on full responsibility for achieving a group's goals, whereas in shared leadership, the leader recognizes that each member has a contribution to make and is willing to share the responsibilities. *Servant leadership* means the leader is there to serve the members of the group and does not use the group to promote personal goals or for personal recognition but instead listens carefully to what the members of the group need and want and acts accordingly. The combination of *shared and servant leadership* is the style that works most effectively for groups of retired people. This is *empowering* leadership.

The personal style of leaders is the approach they take to facilitating a group. Their communications, expressions, and attitudes are a critical part of their style. Their way of relating to and working with older adults results from specific choices with respect to the following factors. *Autonomy* is the amount of freedom a leader grants individuals—the latitude members have for deciding what to do and how to do it. *Responsibility* refers to the degree to which the responsibility for the process is shared by the leader and the group members. (Group process refers to collaboration, cooperation, a feeling of togetherness, and participation of group members.) *Discipline* refers to methods the leader uses to reward or to punish group members for their behavior, contributions, and performance of tasks. *Sharing* is the extent to which leaders reveal themselves to groups and the degree to which group members feel comfortable being honest, admitting weaknesses, and sharing personal experiences and difficulties.

The leader's methods and techniques for working with people in a group are often a matter of personal habit and conviction learned over many years and through a variety of experiences. To a certain degree, they are influenced by conscious choices, by awareness of various styles and techniques available, and by a conscious decision to use one or more of them in a particular group or situation.

The word *group* is used here to mean a number of people who come together with similar aims. People belong to many groups in the course of a lifetime ranging from family, to scouts, to a firm's board of directors, to the PTA. Different groups have different styles of operation and different kinds of leadership. People belong to groups as diverse in style as the following examples:

- An army self-defense workshop in which the trainer behaves like a "benevolent dictator
- An adult education class in which the tutor acts as guide
- A planning team in which the leader acts as catalyst
- A support group where there is in which shared leadership

What happens in groups in the time people spend together pursuing their similar aims can be generally classified under two headings—task process and people process. Task process includes any aspect of behavior that contributes directly to bringing group members closer to their goals. Broadly speaking, the whole business of who does what, why, when, how, and with whom—whether these matters are decided consciously or otherwise—constitutes task process. Anything that happens in connection with any of the following is part of the task process of the group, because these are all procedures connected with how group members will achieve their goals (e.g., planning and preparation, performance, assessment, evaluation, and record-keeping).

The authoritarian leader takes the responsibility for most task-related and people-related decisions. This person decides what work will be carried out and who works with whom, and if there are any problems with difficult members, he or she has a word with them confidentially. The empowering leader hands the responsibility for decisions over to the group. The group decides how the work is done and has its own procedures for addressing differences of opinion and conflict.

As authoritarian leaders give up one kind of responsibility, they take on another. The leader now becomes responsible for making sure that members find ways of dealing with their new responsibilities. The leader becomes more of an enabler or facilitator, rather than an authority. Often, the leader sets the tone for the group, whether consciously or unconsciously. It now becomes the leader's job to bring the changing style of leadership into the open so that decision making can become a group matter.

An autocratic or authoritarian style tends to be typified by statements or questions that are really commands:

- This is a good way to do it.
- Why don't you do it this way?
- Could you just have a look at this?

An empowering style tends to be typified by genuine questions, such as:

- How are we going to tackle this?
- What is the best way to share the work?
- What are we going to do next?

Evaluate your style by asking yourself questions about both the task and behavior aspects of your group.

Task Process

- Who decides what to do next?
- Who decides how it will be done?
- Who decides who will work with whom?
- Who decides how long to spend on each activity?
- Who evaluates completed work?

People Process

- Who deals with people who dominate discussions?
- Who deals with people who antagonize one another?
- Who deals with people who lack commitment?
- Who decides whether it's okay to smoke, be late, interrupt others, and so forth?
- Who deals with people who do not meet expectations?

If you answer "leader" most of the time, your style is autocratic. If you answer "members" to most of the questions, your style is empowering. The bottom line is the people must come first. At any one time there may be members who are heavily dependent on the leader for support and guidance, members who are capable of organizing their own affairs, and others who are somewhere in between. This makes it difficult to achieve a consistent style of leadership. Thus the leader must develop some sensitivity to what style of leadership is appropriate when and learn to adjust personal style in response to the changing needs of the group. The skill of the leader lies in being able to adapt to many different situations.

Leadership style in retirement organizations places its emphasis on people, building relationships, and developing trust. Therefore, an effective style for managers, directors, coordinators, and volunteer leaders is to provide nonauthoritarian direction, inspiration, and motivation. If a leader's style of direction is to make demands or delegate tasks to other volunteers, the leader is usually ineffective; asking and inviting results is more effective leadership. Delegation can be viewed as giving someone the freedom, authority, and responsibility to do the job. If volunteer leaders are to be inspiring and motivating, they first need a healthy dose of leadership and personal development training to meet their own needs. Only then can they work in such a way that others feel needed, productive, and respected.

☐ Leader Language

> Teaching consists in the use of language for the purpose of increasing knowledge. Increase of knowledge depends upon activity internal to the knower and upon divine illumination of the contents of his mind. We employ language as an instrument to prompt others to know, to direct their attention to sensible objects, to activate their memories and their processes of reasoning, and to bring about their perception of truths concerning nature and society. Teaching is this instrumental use of language. Those persons who teach employ language in this way to increase the knowledge of others, but they do not by their speech convey knowledge to anyone. They prompt others only to knowledge which they must come by through a consultation of their own inner experience.
>
> —St. Augustine, 4th century

The challenge is how to change the group's approach from traditional to empowering leadership. This involves moving from a traditional, autocratic style to one in which everyone shares responsibility for leadership. Empowerment does not mean disempowering some people and giving power to others who may not want it and who may lack the knowledge, skills, and attitudes to use it wisely. It means sharing responsibility among group members, giving voice to their perspectives, and supporting their development as leaders.

Transforming the leadership in any group or organization begins with a deeper understanding of the needs, desires, beliefs, and values of the membership. Changes that follow may encompass changing attitudes and beliefs, organizational mandates and structures, and the quality of working relationships. One way of helping to change attitudes and beliefs is to change the language that is used to one that is more supportive and inclusive. People who have the freedom to choose because they are retired are more likely to share the workload if they are invited, encouraged, supported, inspired, and recognized, rather than appointed, delegated, or seconded.

The following list of words and phrases can be used to develop a greater awareness of the language used and to help leaders make changes that reflect and promote self-confident, empowering leadership by communicating certain feelings (e.g., of self-confidence and respect for others).

Dictionary of Leader Language

USED TO SAY . . .	NEED TO SAY . . .
My name is . . .	I am . . .
Ann stole my idea.	I agree with Ann.
Could I support . . . ?	I support . . .
I would like to . . .	I am going to . . .
Pardon me, we are off topic . . .	Let's get back on topic.
Excuse me, can I say something . . .?	I would like to add . . .
I think I'll try to . . .	I'm going to . . .
board of directors	advisory committee
executive director	coordinator
president	chair
conflict	issue
problem	challenge
delegate	ask or invite
lead	serve
volunteers	leaders
criticism	feedback
instruct or teach	facilitate
speech	presentation
call to order	welcome everyone

Effective Communication

1. *Organize your thoughts.* Think through what you plan to say before you say it. Speak the language of the listener. Do not use a 25-cent word when a 5-cent word will do.
2. *Consider the purpose of each communication.* Before you communicate, ask yourself what you really want to accomplish with your message (e.g., obtain information, initiate action). Identify your most important goal and then adapt your language, tone, and approach to serve your objective. Do not try to accomplish too much with each communication. The sharper the focus of your message, the greater its chance of success.
3. *Consult with others.* Frequently it is desirable or necessary to seek the participation of others in planning a communication or developing the facts on which to base it. Such consultation often helps to lend additional insight and objectivity to your message. Moreover, those who have helped you plan your communication will give it their active support.
4. *Take note of overtones and content.* Your tone of voice, your expression, and your apparent receptiveness to the responses of others have tremendous impact on those you wish to reach. Frequently overlooked, these subtleties of communication can affect a listener's reaction to

a message even more than its basic content. Similarly, your choice of language, particularly your awareness of the meaning and emotion in the words you use, predetermines to a large extent the reactions of your listeners.

5. *Convey something helpful.* Consideration for the other person's interests and needs and the habit of trying to look at things from their point of view frequently present opportunities to convey something of immediate benefit or long-range value. People are most responsive to others whose messages take their own interests into account.

6. *Courage goes a long way.* Although communications may be aimed primarily at meeting the demands of an immediate situation, it is not easy to communicate frankly on such matters as poor performance or the shortcomings of a committee chairperson, but postponing disagreeable communications makes them more difficult in the long run and is actually unfair to other members and to the group.

7. *Have your actions support communication.* In the final analysis, the most persuasive kind of communication is not what you say, but what you do. When a person's action or attitudes contradict their words, we tend to discount what they have said.

8. *Body language.* Notice the actual physical distance at which you feel comfortable communicating with various individuals (e.g., strangers, associates, friends, authority figures). How much eye contact do you maintain when talking and when listening? What do you do with your hands? your feet? your posture? your breathing? What does this body language communicate about you to others and about them to you?

9. *The other person's place.* Empathy means entering another person's world, walking a mile in their shoes, seeing things through their eyes. It is an attitude of moving out of ourselves to understand the feelings of another and has an important effect on the quality of communication.

10. *Be a listener.* First seek to understand, then to be understood. When we begin speaking, we often cease to listen in the larger sense of being attuned to the other person's unspoken reactions and attitudes. An even more serious fact that we are all guilty, at times, of inattentiveness when others are attempting to communicate to us. Listening is one of the most important, most difficult, and most neglected skills in communication. It demands that we concentrate not only on the explicit meanings another person is expressing but on the implicit meanings, unspoken words, and undertones that may be far more significant. We must learn to listen with an inner ear if we are to know the inner person.

Two men were walking along a crowded sidewalk in a downtown business area. Suddenly one exclaimed, "Listen to the lovely sound of that cricket." But the other could not hear. He asked his companion how he could detect the sound of a cricket amid the din of people and traffic. The first man, who was a zoologist, had trained himself to listen to the voices of nature. But he didn't explain. He simply took a coin out of his pocket and dropped it to the sidewalk, whereupon a dozen people began to look about them. "We hear," he said, "what we listen for."

—Kermit L. Long

Motivating, Encouraging, and Supporting

Kotter (1990) has observed,

Motivation and inspiration energize people, not by pushing them in the right direction as control mechanisms do but by satisfying basic human needs for achievement, a sense of belonging, recognition, self-esteem, a feeling of control over one's life, and the ability to live up to one's ideals.

One of the most critical skills for leaders is the ability to motivate others. Motivation of older adults happens mainly through encouragement and challenge. Some years ago, a leadership course was offered at a seniors' center. After the course, some participants started a drama group. We asked what a drama group had to do with leadership. They replied, "It's personal development, getting things done, acting as a role model, and dealing with problems. It's communicating with people, leading them to a goal. Leadership, like drama, is a way of life, not just part of it." Through a leadership-training program, these seniors were motivated because they were given opportunities to get what they wanted. What was it they wanted? They reflected,

We have traveled into many different areas and have seen people blossom. We live better, speak better, feel better, like ourselves better and we are serving others. It's amazing what it has done for us and it all began with a leadership-training program.

Seniors as a group are underrepresented in volunteer programs across the country, and senior volunteers are generally reluctant to commit themselves to leadership roles. Anyone who has ever worked with volunteers is aware of the critical importance of meeting the needs of the individual to find and keep volunteers.

Seniors are not just volunteers who are older, many are volunteers or potential volunteers for the first time in their lives, and these senior volunteers have some unique needs. If we expect to harness their skills and talents for their personal benefit and for the benefit of groups, organizations, and communities, understanding their needs becomes paramount.

Retired people need a sense of purpose, to feel worthwhile, and to be recognized. They also need to relax and enjoy life. Those who have worked hard all their lives may see retirement as a time to have fun, to be spontaneous, and to be free of major responsibilities. For those who were denied an education in younger years or who devoted their lives to caring for others, retirement may be the time to pursue learning and personal development. They want to make the time count, particularly if they have been in demanding management roles most of their lives or if they have looked after 42 children and cooked 35,782 meals.

For many people, retirement from the work force or from family responsibilities after the death of a spouse may be the first time in their lives that they actually have the freedom to choose what they would like to do. They may choose to become leaders or they may choose not to become leaders. They may choose to spend the rest of their life knitting.

How can their experience and skill be harnessed? First, leaders can understand the needs of retired people and create options that give them a sense of purpose and of making a contribution, while adding fun and enjoyment to their lives. Second, leaders can expand the definition of leadership to incorporate many roles and responsibilities so everyone can be seen as having a contribution to make. Third, leaders need to demonstrate and develop shared–servant leadership. Finally, providing quality training programs to meet the needs of retired persons is critical to success—programs that recognize and build on seniors' individual skills and knowledge, provide fun and enjoyment, conserve and create energy, make good use of time, and present opportunities for personal development and a meaningful contribution to the community.

When asked what motivated them to take on leadership roles, senior volunteers said,

- An opportunity for self-expression.
- Some of us have a need for power and status—others don't.
- We are simply willing horses when no one else will do the job.
- We get involved because we care for others.
- We have ideas and enjoy seeing them put into practice.
- Satisfaction comes from making things happen.
- We want a challenge.
- We want to keep our minds stimulated and healthy.
- We want to stay involved and use our experience and talents.

In every organization that uses volunteers, the greatest challenge is getting and keeping people involved. Directors, coordinators, and managers are all seeking ways to motivate current volunteers and the hundreds of others on standby, many just waiting to be asked or to be told they are needed. All effective leaders want to tap the unrealized potential of this vast human resource. Beyond that, exceptional leaders want to transform people, enabling them to become the best they can be. Many managers think of motivation as something volunteers bring to the task and therefore have never thought of motivating others as part of their job. When it comes to making an organization run well with happy, healthy staff and volunteers, motivation is everything.

Certainly some motivation must come from within, but most people perform at higher levels and stay committed and involved when the manager is empowering—that is, gives power away. When this happens, leaders gain more power and a wonderful stream of reciprocity follows. No one has the power—and everyone does. When people are empowered, they go well beyond what is expected of them and what they expect of themselves. This is what motivation is about. When volunteers feel empowered, their self-esteem increases, they have new found confidence, they are enthusiastic and vital. "People are nourished by transforming work, growth, reaching their potential. . . . Only by continually renewing its members can an organization continually renew itself" (DePree, 1997, p. 105). This transformation is the secret to success

This process begins by becoming familiar with human needs—by finding out what volunteers need and helping them meet their needs. People are often motivated by something they want that they do not have. Individuals are driven or motivated to fill this gap or discrepancy. This driving force causes people to act. It is important to look at what people need, because that is what they want.

A motivating leader

- Creates an atmosphere of respect and trust
- Knows that volunteers need to feel significant, to belong, to contribute
- Knows how to open up creativity in others and is open to new ideas
- Builds team members by recognizing individual potential
- Lifts people to their higher selves by giving meaning to what they do
- Expects the best in others and has a standard of excellence
- Is an optimist and encourages others to be the same
- Believes that individuals have something special to offer and can contribute in a unique way
- Knows how to listen
- Has genuine respect and belief in the abilities of older adults
- Has a sense of humor
- Is interested in the lives of members
- Provides ongoing recognition, pointing out things people do well and recognizing that their contribution is meaningful and important
- Gives reassurance and support to people in new positions
- Involves individuals and groups in decision making
- Encourages personal development
- Emphasizes cooperation over competition

- Makes quality leadership training a priority for individuals and groups to bring out the best skills, talents, and abilities
- Treats people like they already have what it takes to do the job
- Models all aspects of effective leadership

How did we go from the concept of wants to the concept of human needs? Simply by realizing that a person wants to satisfy a perceived need. If I am hungry, I have a need and I want to satisfy it by eating. If I am tired, I have a perceived need and I want to satisfy it by sleeping. If I am lonely, I have a perceived need for human contact and I want to satisfy it by experiencing some companionship.

☐ Maslow's Hierarchy of Human Needs

Maslow's hierarchy is based on a number of premises. First, human needs arrange themselves in a hierarchy, and the emergence of one need is based on satisfaction of a more basic need. Second, humans always want and are never satisfied. Third, no need is discrete in that it is based on the satisfaction of a previous need. In other words, we may experience more than one need at the same time. And finally, needs differ between individuals and groups at any given time.

Maslow has organized human needs into a hierarchy that helps us to understand behavior. This hierarchy describes five basic needs: *Physical* needs are the needs of the body for food, water, shelter and clothing. Humans, like most other animals, have a strong drive toward self-preservation. Satisfaction of these needs is necessary for survival. *Security* needs are of two types: physical security (i.e., a desire to be safe from personal harm) and economic security. Economic security is the desire to reach a reasonable economic level and then not to worry about loss of income because of old age, loss of job, accident, and so forth. Thus, the desire is to avoid both present harm and the threat of future harm. *Social* needs refer to the need to feel a sense of belonging, that one is an accepted member of a group and an integral part of the organization to which one belongs. *Esteem* needs represent the ego in operation and include such things as status, recognition, prestige, and self-respect. *Self-actualization* is the need to feel that one is making progress toward reaching one's full potential, whatever that may be, that the individual is doing what best reflects their skills and activities, that they are doing what they should and want to be doing. Needs at lower levels must be satisfied first (e.g., physical comfort before challenges). If needs in one area are not met, it is difficult to move up; if physical safety is threatened, it is difficult to feel positive self-esteem or to develop one's full potential.

How does Maslow's hierarchy apply to the question of leadership and motivation? First, it provides a structure for understanding why people do things, why some people seem to be caught at a certain level of development and cannot proceed beyond it. Second, the theory provides a basis for understanding some of the dynamics that operate in a group and perhaps a new point of view for dealing with people. If some members of the group are stuck at the level of concern for personal safety and security, it is unlikely that they will be able to function effectively in social settings that require them to move beyond that level. Third, this theory helps us see motivation in a new way. The traditional ideas, that people worked to provide money, food, and a roof over their heads need to be revised in the light of this hierarchy of needs. If basic physical needs are met, they are no longer a concern; and people become more interested in higher needs, such as job satisfaction, recognition for effort, and an opportunity to learn and meet new challenges.

Traditionally, we have been very informal about placing volunteers in suitable jobs: either we ask someone who has already done the job before and has done it well or we ask "who will contact the media about new releases?" and hope that someone will step forward, someone who knows how to carry out the tasks for which they have volunteered. Using Maslow's hierarchy of needs can help us to match the needs of our volunteers with the tasks that our group needs to accomplish. Make a list of all the activities that are performed by volunteers and then sort them into clusters depending on how much responsibility is required to complete them. Refer to Maslow's hierarchy to determine which of your volunteers' needs are most likely to be met by doing each of these tasks.

Some volunteers like the security of routine, structured work; they may need to be given tasks where the level of responsibility is low. Others volunteer for social reasons: give this volunteer a stack of letters to stuff into envelopes at home and you may never see her again. Instead, organize a "work bee" where volunteers who need to socialize can work together, even if it is a boring task such as stuffing envelopes. Better yet, find her people-oriented work, like making phone calls or greeting guests. Some volunteers like a more demanding role. Identify the most responsible activities and give these to people who will find that the responsibility is a challenge. Although this approach takes more time and thought, it repays your efforts by showing volunteers that you recognize and are concerned about their needs.

Motivation is the process of influencing the feelings and ideas of others to create a positive attitude toward a given task or longer term activity. As a result of this positive shift of attitude, the behavior of participants will change, indicated by signs of enjoyment of activities (smiles, laughter), greater initiative, acceptance of responsibility, and so forth. Motivation is what causes people to act, to perform, to want to do something.

Everyone has different incentives based on their individual needs, and it is crucial to recognize this when working with people.

There is no one way to motivate people. As a group leader, motivating people to accomplish the goals of the group is one of the main challenges. There are, however, some universally accepted principles that, if applied correctly, always result in increased motivation. Motivation is a matter of human understanding. It becomes a process of encouraging people to go as far as possible toward reaching their hopes and dreams and helping them achieve their full potential. This requires giving people opportunities to show what they can do and recognizing their efforts. They must be made to feel wanted, and this can be done by making them aware of how their efforts contribute to the group or organization. A motivating leader attempts to understand people, to help and support them in achieving their aims, so that they know that they can count on the support of others in return. And so it is with motivation in a group. Leaders who are genuinely concerned about each member of the group can supply a great amount of encouragement and support.

It is important to an older person to know that their life experience and skills can still be useful in the community. If individuals feel they can no longer be of use to their family or community, self-esteem diminishes and depression may follow. An effective leader will assess the person's most likely area of contribution to the group and ask them to take over some responsibility in that area. The leader then acknowledges a great idea or a job well done and gives recognition in a way that makes the person feel valued and useful.

Inspiring others builds motivation in them. A motivated person is a person who desires something. Leaders motivate people by tapping into their basic motivational needs. Retired volunteers have needs that center around self-esteem and self-confidence. Many lost confidence when they lost a spouse or left the workplace. Built into every volunteer activity, job, and program must be the opportunity for developing and maintaining self-esteem and confidence. When a person's self-esteem is lowered by a credible person (such as a group leader), the participant tends to become defensive and any discussion becomes nonproductive. By maintaining or enhancing the individual's self-esteem, the discussion becomes more productive as the person becomes more open and helpful. Self-esteem is enhanced when the leader treats the participant as though they are competent. An active belief and interest in people's skills and individual development is another way of enhancing self-esteem. An effective leader must continually recognize effort—from verbal praise, to creating opportunities for volunteers to associate with or meet VIPs, to offering quality training programs, to formal awards. Older adults need opportunities for personal development and for learning new things. They are more likely to feel they are getting somewhere and keeping up with the fast changing world.

Some theories of motivation stress that motivation is associated with perceived rewards to the individual. In groups, the main reward is personal growth. By consistently referring to the benefits and relationship between task and process, a group leader can contribute to the motivation of members and thus achieve the group's goals. When leaders help members to meet their needs, they are motivating those people; when someone is motivated, there will be a positive response. It is this positive response that indicates a high level of commitment. Being committed to a group means being committed to achieving a common goal. The task of a group leader is to motivate members to commit their energy toward the achievement of the group's goals. When one approach does not work, a second must be tried, then a third. This is the leader's responsibility and greatest challenge.

Senior volunteers have a need for achievement. They need to be challenged, believed in, and given something to accomplish. Older people need something to feel proud of, they want to feel successful. To develop motivation and commitment, both individual and group needs must be met. Empowering leaders believe in the potential of members and in the group as a whole. They focus on providing opportunities that are relevant, enjoyable, challenging, and different. By encouraging people to assess their personal contribution to the group and their goals for the future, the group leader can generate enthusiasm and a spirit of cooperation. Progress means building on small changes and improvements, while maintaining the balance between the needs of individuals and the goals of the group.

Having a sense of control and being part of a decision making team are critical needs of older adults. A leader motivates people by empowering them. Participants like to be asked for their input in solving problems and to be involved in the decisions that affect group life and activities. In all situations, people can and should have input into the decision-making process. Participants themselves are often closest to the issue and can offer the most qualified solution.

Finally, retired volunteers need a sense of belonging, an opportunity to be part of a group or effective team that is making a difference in the community. This sense of belonging creates positive feelings for those involved in groups, which in turn spreads to other individuals and groups, motivating them to become involved. Volunteer work must be stimulating, interesting, challenging and above all fun. Enticing people with goals and believing in their worth excites and energizes them, motivating them to be even more successful. Ultimately, people become healthier as they begin to accept their successes. They feel competent, they feel significant, they feel confident—all because they have been motivated. Ultimately, they will then be able to motivate their peers, and the circle will be complete.

Motivating and encouraging leaders attend to the physical comfort of the group and help each individual feel a sense of belonging. They build trust and create a safe environment for members to express themselves freely. They create an atmosphere of mutual understanding and respect, one that recognizes potential. They have the skills to persuade difficult people to return to the issue at hand, to use group members to find solutions. They believe that people come first and the task comes second. They involve everyone in the group, while maintaining a sense of optimism and a belief that whatever they set out to do can and will be done.

9
CHAPTER

Back to New Basics

There are times when neither the teacher nor the student knows for sure what's going to happen. In the beginning, there's a safe environment that enables people to be really open and to learn and to listen to each other's ideas. Then comes brainstorming, where the spirit of evaluation is subordinated to the spirit of creativity, imagining, and intellectual networking. Then an absolutely unusual phenomenon begins to take place. The entire class is transformed with the excitement of a new thrust, a new idea, a new direction that's hard to define.

—Covey, 1989, p. 265

☐ Facilitating Learning: The Three E's

The opportunity to learn new skills or to enhance what people already know can add immeasurably to the richness of life in later years. Learning, however, is different in retirement, not because of age but because of the many diverse experiences that have shaped beliefs, attitudes, and personal identity. Helping people build on life experience as part of the learning process requires great sensitivity and skill. In fact, the skill of the workshop leader seems to be the most important feature of a successful workshop. It is a time when all older adults, many of whom have not been well served by education in the past, have the opportunity to participate in the best learning experiences. This chapter summarizes old information that needs to be reemphasized. Based on discussions and studies with older learners in seniors' centers and organizations, community colleges, and universities throughout the Western world, new insights have been added (e.g., how to build on life experience and how to create energy in a group).

Introduction to Learning and Teaching

Many people believe that a good teacher can teach anyone anything. If you know how to teach, you can teach any age group—provided you know the subject and the group. As soon as teachers know the level of knowledge in the group, they often proceed according to universal principles to fill the gaps in information. It all sounds very simple. But the truth is that some people are more effective as instructors of older adults than others.

Many instructors hesitate to set older adults apart as a special learning group even though they will admit older learners have special needs. They fear that they might reinforce negative stereotypes of older students as being less able to learn. This is not so. Knowledge about older adult learners is critical to effective learning and teaching.

Characterisitics of Adult Learners

In comparison with children, adults are considered to be more problem centered, self-directed, and independent in their approach to learning (Knowles, 1980). But that is not always the case. Some claim adult learners are ambivalent; they want to be dependent and independent at the same time. They seek expert knowledge but want to make their own decisions and do not want other people telling them what to do. Adult learners have many roles and responsibilities and pass through a number of life stages, each new stage stimulating a reinterpretation of past experience. They have distinct preferences for methods of learning and experience anxiety and ambivalence toward learning.

A useful way of approaching adult learners is to focus on the variety and diversity of their experience and to find ways to integrate past experience and create positive attitudes toward learning. But first, clarification exactly what is meant by "older" is in order. It has been said that old is a relative concept and usually means 15 years older than we are. For the purposes of this book, anyone over 50 years of age is included for the simple reason that 50 is the minimum age of membership in many seniors' community centers.

> What is meant by aging and being old? The youngest person I know is Elsie, who at 82 has just started her B.A. degree. The oldest person I know

is Robert, age 32. He knows everything about everything. He hasn't room for one new idea. His mind is made up. His life is over. So, although he thinks he is quite young, those of us around him know he is very, very old. (Battersby, 1989, p. 28)

One particular aspect of aging is worth stressing here. It has been shown that age, as such, has nothing to do with the ability to learn. People can learn at any age—if they want to. What characteristics distinguish an older learning group? The most outstanding feature is its diversity. Paradoxically, the single characteristic that distinguishes an old adult learning group from any other group is the diversity of individuals with respect to education, life experience, social status, income, and health (Snider & Ceridwyn, 1986).

Who is the Older Adult Learner?

Aside from diversity, there are characteristics of older adults learners that are useful to know. Older adults

- Can learn at any age
- Become more different from each other as they age
- Have vast stores of knowledge and experience
- Must see that learning is relevant to them
- Learn by reflecting on past experience
- Are motivated to learn by a myriad of of their own reasons
- May have sensory changes that interfere with learning
- Need a safe, accepting environment
- Need extra time to integrate new ideas
- Sometimes worry that they may be losing their memory
- Want to be independent and make their own decisions
- Often have negative attitudes toward formal education
- Like to learn from an expert

These points are discussed here as they relate to leadership and personal development programs in terms of the three Es of older learners: experience, education, and expectations.

Experience

What is different about older learners?, the response is, the wealth of life experience they bring to every learning situation. Furthermore, leadership has been part of their everyday experience, although many are unaware of it. Their concept of leadership, personal leadership style, and attitudes toward leadership have been shaped over a lifetime in the home, in the workplace, and in community life.

Not only do older adults have a lifetime of experience related to leaders they have known and loved, many of them have been leaders themselves—presidents, managers, matrons, superintendents, administrators, foremen. Many others have served in leadership roles in their family networks, church groups, or volunteer activities and probably have a variety of leadership skills even though they never thought of themselves as leaders. Many participants are currently in a variety of leadership roles both in the community and in their family networks. In their personal lives, some may have the added burden of caring for elderly parents, grandchildren, or an ailing spouse.

Apart from all this, older people are free to choose how they wish to spend their leisure time. They are people who may be searching for new experiences or new roles. The transition from work or family responsibilities to leisure and retirement activities often prompts them to seek out new opportunities. Some may be looking for ways to continue using their skills and experience; others may be exploring undeveloped skills and talents. They are searching for new ways to feel good and to feel worthwhile. Is there anyone left out there who still thinks older adults are rigid and set in their ways and just want to go to Florida or Palm Springs for the rest of their lives?

Education

To this new opportunity for self-development, older adults bring a lifetime of educational experience. Individual histories may range from those who have never been educated in an English-speaking country to those with an eighth-grade education, to those with a university degree. Regardless of the level of education, many were never excited about education. Formal education taught them many facts that were not useful in the real world; life experience was the real teacher. Studying history never taught anyone how to feed a family during the Depression.

Furthermore, the experiences they had may have left them with a series of restricting beliefs (e.g., learning is a painful process and involves a lot of memory work) and inadequate training for making decisions. The teacher was the authority who administered knowledge, and the student's task was to remember it and spill it out at examination time. And if learning is associated with remembering information and facts, and people believe their memory declines as they get older, they may well be anxious about undertaking any activity classified as educational.

Expectations

Older learners generally expect education to be information given by experts and presented in the form of a talk or lecture, and they often expect to be less able to learn than when they were younger. Not long ago, we had lunch with a mature student at the university. He reflected on his first semester after being away from school for some time; he had worked as a writer for television and going back into the classroom was scary for him. He said all the other students looked like kids and he felt different. He was worried that he would not be able to remember things as well as the others who were much younger. He was 26.

Another woman, aged 35, returning to the classroom after an absence of 15 years and had precisely the same anxieties about a declining ability to learn. She now has a PhD at the age of 50 and no longer has any doubt about her ability to compete with kids in the classroom.

We also recall a man in his 70s who lived in a retirement complex. Music was his hobby and he enjoyed entertaining the residents. From time to time, he traveled downtown by bus to purchase new musical arrangements, a trip that took about 20 minutes. By the time he arrived home, he would have the entire musical score committed to memory. He never had a memory problem.

It is not our intention to dismiss the anxiety about decline in learning ability and memory that most older adults experience. However, recent research shows that retired persons can learn as easily as anyone else if the task has meaning for them and if they are not pressured. In the final analysis, it seems the anxiety about memory loss may be the most important factor. In other words, no matter how old people are, when they are anxious they do not remember things as well. Individual and collective strength lies in a rich diversity of life experiences. The challenge is to create positive attitudes toward learning by acknowledging and building on life experience.

Strategies to Enhance Learning

Education Redefined

Traditional concepts of education as the accumulation of new bits of information or preparation for a profession do not usually apply to learning in later life. Therefore, education must be redefined before strategies for enhancing learning are discussed. The purpose of education is to help people use both experience and knowledge to their own ends, whether for self-fulfillment, or personal growth or to develop specific skills.

Retirement is a stage of life characterized by freedom, time to engage in activities for their own sake, and self-enrichment and personal development. For many women, retirement may mean freedom from the primary role that comes with the loss of a spouse.

Learning in retirement must blend knowledge and life experience and must be personal, practical, and participatory. As one senior said, "Learning needs to be more a stepping outside ourselves, becoming a part of our community. . . . It involves sharing of experiences, not back to kindergarten." Teaching in this context has little to do with presenting expert knowledge. The teacher's role is one of facilitator of learning rather than transmitter of information and facts. A facilitator is someone who helps people to learn what they want to know and to clarify and share knowledge they already have. In this sense, the relationship between facilitator and learner is one of equal participation in a shared learning enterprise.

Although the role of teacher as expert authority may still be appropriate in some cases (e.g., in teaching introductory computer skills), it is seldom appropriate when expert knowledge is derived from everyday experience. Individual participants in leadership-training programs may well have more expert knowledge than the facilitator, and collectively they most certainly do.

Some students prefer a traditional teaching format simply because they are most familiar with it, but it is essential that they be gently led toward a more participatory sharing of experience and ideas. It is through participation that individuals develop an appreciation for the value of their own life experience and the confidence to speak up and share that experience with others. To go one step further, it is through shared learning that teacher and student can work toward the ultimate goal, shared leadership. Clearly, the teacher's primary role in this enterprise is to facilitate individual development. There are a variety of words (e.g., *teacher, educator, instructor, trainer*) that describe the person in charge of learning, but henceforth that person will be referred to as the facilitator or workshop leader.

Given the focus on helping individuals make use of their own experience, the facilitator's job is to plan activities and lead group discussions that connect new information with life experience. What follows are practical tips on learning in retirement, using life experience, and presenting new information, beginning with the technical adaptations, because they are key. There is no point using sophisticated discussion methods to incorporate life experiences if no one can hear you.

☐ Technical Adaptations for Older Adult Learners

The longer most of us sit, lie or stand still, the harder it is for us to stay conscious, to think creatively, or to keep vital. Environments should be designed to allow for the greatest possible variety and freedom of movements. (McCay, 1973, p. 59)

Group situations may be particularly stressful for those whose hearing and vision are impaired or whose energy may be reduced by disability or illness. Creating a comfortable learning environment reduces unnecessary stress, conserves energy, and facilitates learning. Some of the important considerations are matters of common sense, yet often they are not given proper attention. The following strategies are essential for any learning group of retired persons.

To compensate for hearing loss:

1. Use a microphone when appropriate.
2. Speak in a loud voice with clear diction and maintain lower pitch.
3. Face your audience with as much light on your face as possible to facilitate lip reading and decrease glare.
4. Choose a place where background noise is at a minimum.
5. Secure attention before speaking.
6. Encourage constant checks and feedback from the audience.
7. Position the group so each member can be seen and heard.

To compensate for poor eyesight:

1. Allow participants to adjust lighting, to move around, and so forth.
2. Provide maximal lighting.
3. Use larger print for all written materials.
4. If showing a movie, allow time for light and dark adaptation.
5. Use primary colors in presentations (e.g., combinations of blue and green are difficult to distinguish.

To conserve energy:

1. Control outside distractions.
2. Allow for reduced energy levels in participants.
3. Pay special attention to physical comfort (e.g., heat, air circulation, chairs). Discomfort creates fatigue.
4. Schedule sessions when energy is highest (e.g., morning sessions are best for most older adults).
5. Use a variety of teaching methods.
6 Use active learning wherever possible (e.g., have people move in and out of small groups or writing on flip charts.
7. Be sure total time is not too long (2 1/2—3 hours is the maximum to allow for a workshop).

8. Allow for short nutrition and energy breaks.

To communicate with someone who is hard of hearing:

1. It is important to have the person's attention before speaking. Because people who are hard of hearing cannot hear the usual call to attention, they may need a tap on the shoulder, a wave of the hands, or other visual signals to gain attention.
2. Look directly at the person while speaking. Even a slight turn of the head can obscure a person's vision. Other distracting factors that affect communication include moustaches, which, obscures the lips and habits such as smoking, pencil chewing, and putting one's hands in front of one's face.
3. Speak slowly and clearly, but do not exaggerate or overemphasize words. This distorts lip movements, making lipreading more difficult.
4. Pantomime, body language and facial expression are important factors in communication. Be sure to use all of them.
5. Try to maintain eye contact with people who are hard of hearing. Eye contact helps convey the feeling of direct communication.
6. Try to rephrase a thought rather than repeating the same words. Sometimes a group of lip movements is difficult to lipread. If the person does not understand, try to restate the sentence.
7. Do not be embarrassed about communicating through paper and pencil. Getting the message across is more important than the medium.
8. In communicating with a person who is hard of hearing, it is a good idea to remember that intelligence, personality, age at onset of deafness, language background, listening skills, lip reading, and speech abilities all vary with each deaf person, just as the skills and personality of each person vary.
9. The hearing impaired person's understanding of conversation is a shared responsibility.
10. Most hearing problems do not benefit from loudness, so it does not help to shout to someone wearing a hearing aid.
11. Other people's accents are a challenge for the hearing impaired person. If you have an accent, be ready to use a pen and paper.
12. At parties or meetings, do not limit the conversations to essentials or niceties. It can be frustrating for a person to be without the chance to join in.
13. Accusations that persons who have hearing loss hear only what they want to are unjust. To pick up information, they have to concentrate harder and therefore tire easily. In actuality, they do hear only what they can. When tired, distracted, or ill, they are less able to hear and understand. Ability to hear changes with each situation.
14. Impatience with another's listening behavior will not help; it only causes them to tense up and hear less. The more relaxed and accepted the person feels, the better the communication.
15. Find out if one ear functions better then the other and speak to that side.

16. A deadpan face is difficult. Remember that the tone of voice may not be heard, so use your acting powers to help project the meaning.

17. Hearing aids do not restore hearing completely. They amplify sound and increase the distance from which the wearer can hear, but they cannot restore lost frequencies. Be prepared for confusions, and help your friend to laugh at them.

18. Hearing loss need not mean loss of fun. Theater, music, and dancing can all, with a little forethought, still be part of life.

19. Loss can bring loneliness to the hard-of-hearing. Too often they begin to feel isolated. Too often others stop talking to them or feel embarrassed with them simply because they do not know how much was heard. A little informed courtesy can make the loss seem less.

20. Be aware of possible emotional responses such as embarrassment, denial, anger, frustration, disorientation, or confusion.

21. Begin every conversation by positioning yourself close to and in front of the person. This will help him or her relax and know that you care by the effort that you are making.

22. If you are not being understood, ask the person what you can do differently.

23. From time to time ask the person how well you are doing. Positive comments will make you feel appreciated for your effort.

24. A pad of paper and pencil are often necessary for writing down key words or phrases. Be aware, however, of elderly persons who cannot read and who may be too embarrassed to tell you.

25. Candlelight dinners are not a treat for a hard-of-hearing person who cannot see your face. They need to see your face to lipread. Also they cannot eat their food while it is hot if they are watching you talk.

26. Take time to include person with hearing loss in a group situation; they feel hurt and frustrated because of missing so much.

27. Do not talk to the hard-of-hearing person's companion just because it is easier. Try several different ways of communicating with the person until you find one or a combination of ways that work.

28. Most important of all, do not give up. If you give up trying to communicate, you have given up on the person.

Using Life Experience

To adults, life experience is who they are; devaluing life experience devalues them as persons. Life experience must be both acknowledged and incorporated into new learning for the following reasons:

- It gives individuals a sense of self-worth and reinforces the value of their personal experiences.
- To be meaningful, new learning must connect with past life experience.
- Adults are motivated to learn material that relates to their present roles and tasks.

One of the great contributions of education to the quality of life in retirement is in helping older adults make sense of their life experiences. Learning new material is easier when it makes sense to the individual and it is connected with personal experience. This involves using life experience in a variety of ways. It includes providing opportunities to acknowledge, reflect on, examine, and clarify individual experience; to share experiences with others; and often to reinterpret that experience in light of new information and the shared experiences of others. It is through reflecting on past experience in relation to new material that individuals are able to incorporate new information and deepen their understanding of any topic.

There is often a conflict between the relative values of personal life experience and formal knowledge. Many people are intimidated by so-called experts who tend to devalue personal life experience. This denies them the opportunity to feel good about what they have done and what they can do. It is understandable that when one is young, formal knowledge is more important because there is much less life experience from which to draw. But when one is older, life experience becomes a potentially rich resource for learning.

Whether the emphasis is on formal knowledge or personal experience depends on what is being discussed. Certainly, life experience working on a farm in Saskatchewan has little relevance to an introductory computer class. On the other hand, humanities courses may draw heavily on life experience. A professor teaching a course in history will find that the personal experiences of senior students contribute a rich spontaneous oral history and add a valuable dimension to the educational experiences of their classmates.

Wherever personal life experience is relevant (e.g., in the study of aging, history, communication, leadership), the recounting and reinterpretation of past experience is important even if it is time-consuming. One very common criticism in workshop evaluations of leadership training programs is "not enough time for discussion". That does not mean chitchat, it means fostering the ideas and suggestions being expressed, and making sure there is continuity, flow, and eventually new meaning to the given topic.

☐ Principles of Adult Learning

Principles are laws that are foundational to the way things work. They are fundamental laws that are believed to be true and from which other truths are derived that guide human behavior and help to achieve goals.

These principles of adult learning are key factors in facilitating adult learning. They also relate to the subject, the speaker, the environment, and the presentation of information.

Adults learn best when

- The subject interests them, addresses a particular need, or is useful for them to know.
- The speaker is enthusiastic and knowledgeable about the subject.
- The speaker uses language that is clear and easily understood.
- The environment is conducive to learning—that is, comfortable both physically and emotionally.
- They are treated with respect—their questions encouraged and their comments recognized.
- They know their roles and responsibilities.
- The information is introduced, sequenced, and concluded appropriately.
- The information is related to their experience and builds on prior knowledge.
- Information is presented in a variety of ways—such as, mini-lectures, handouts, notes, discussion, and group work.
- Learning is experiential—that is, learners are active participants in contributing their knowledge and experience and developing new understanding.
- The speaker delivers the message within the allotted time, reinforcing the points without going on and on.
- They have opportunities to critically reflect on and discuss the information presented.

☐ Principles of Leadership: The Secrets of Goose Leadership

In discovering the principles of leadership, the natural laws of Canadian geese provide a metaphor. These "gooseprints" are the secrets of leadership that give geese and people the lift and energy needed to get them off the ground and keep them going in the right direction.

1. To get the show on the road and the geese off the ground, one goose rises into the air and others fall into formation behind.

   - Every group needs a leader to provide the initial inspiration and vision to get an idea off the ground. The primary role of the leader is to inspire and motivate others.

2. Geese always fly in flocks.

- Just like geese, people naturally want to be part of a team, and they want to be full participating members of society

3. Every goose volunteers to take a turn flying in lead position at the apex of the *V*-formation.

   - *V.* is for volunteer, and every volunteer is a potential leader, who is capable of assuming the leadership role when needed.

4. Geese travel a specific and extraordinarily ambitious flight path that is instinctual—and part of their nature as geese.

   - Just as geese have fundamental instincts, it is human instinct to want to achieve one's human potential. Seniors do not become less human as they age, they become more and more in touch with their essential nature as human beings, their connections with the universe, the purpose in their lives. Achieving great heights and making a difference in the world takes energy and commitment—if we settle for less, we will not reap the rewards and satisfactions that follow.

5. Geese are great communicators: they honk to tell the flock about food, where to land, and which way to go.

   - The health of the group is everyone's business. Everyone needs a voice, and everyone needs to be heard.

6. Geese honk from behind to offer encouragement to the leader.

   - Every member of a group needs recognition for their contribution and achievements, and everyone needs encouragement to share the leadership.

7. Geese honk from behind to warn the leaders of danger.

   - Every group member needs to take responsibility for maintaining the health of the group, and for helping to identify and solve group problems. Sharing the problems means sharing the power.

8. When a goose is injured or sick, two geese fall back down to earth and stay with it until it either recovers or dies. Only then do they rise to join another flock of geese on the move.

   - People are more important than the task. Senior leaders often die in the harness or, as we say, in full flight: death is a natural part of leadership. Sincere care and concern for others is essential. Helping others in their hour of greatest need is all part of effective leadership.

☐ How to Conduct Effective Workshops

A workshop is a special learning experience that brings people together around a topic of mutual interest. It engages them actively in processing new information, reinterpreting what they already know, and making it personally relevant. This requires a trained and skillful facilitator.

What makes a workshop work? When workshops are effective, people leave enriched and energized. Poorly facilitated workshops are a waste of time and leave people feeling exhausted. Two critical aspects that make workshops successful are the skill of the workshop leader and his or her ability to create group energy. Some general principles for conducting effective workshops follow.

The Principles

1. Retired persons have a wealth of experience. Effective workshops help participants convert their experience into learning.
2. Retired persons have specific physical needs. Effective workshops have appropriate chairs and tables.
3. Retired persons have well-established habits and preferences. Some like coffee, some hate it; some like tea, some like health drinks, some like a raucous joke, some do not. Effective workshops attempt to meet diverse needs.
4. Retired persons like to be' independent. Effective workshops allow them opportunities to take on greater responsibility for themselves and group leadership.
5. Retired persons like to make good use of their time. Effective workshops use time efficiently.
6. Retired persons have established values and attitudes. Effective workshops respect these, while offering an opportunity to change, if necessary.
7. Retired persons have experienced many changes and losses. Effective workshops build confidence in trying new things and learning to live again.
8. Retired persons like to see what they are learning. Effective workshops provide handouts that reinforce important concepts and information.
9. Retired persons have their own perspective. Effective workshops address issues from the perspective of retirement, not the workplace.

☐ The Role of the Workshop Leader

Facilitators play a variety of roles in helping people to learn. They must have expert knowledge of both the subject and adult learning. They must also have training and experience in how to share that expertise with retired people. They will use a repertoire of skills to stimulate dialogue and discussion, drawing on the resources and the experience of the group and helping to transform that experience and knowledge so that it becomes meaningful to each member of the group.

Conducting an effective workshop requires more than just skilled facilitation. While stimulating participants to contribute their personal knowledge and expertise and to become involved, the facilitator has the opportunity to model effective leadership skills. For example, an effective workshop leader must be skilled at building confidence, communicating, listening, motivating, and supporting others. Being particularly skilled in working with groups, that person is able to inject extra energy and enthusiasm that may continue to gather momentum long after the program is over.

An effective workshop leader

- Is largely responsible for setting the initial climate
- Is genuinely interested in the topic
- Communicates respect for each individual
- Regards both self and participants as resources for learning
- Supports participants' efforts and encourages new behaviors
- Provides useful and timely feedback and recalls events, interactions, and discussions accurately
- Acknowledges new ideas and emphasizes and repeats what is valued
- Models desirable attitudes and behaviors
- Challenges and probes
- Has a sense of humor

Conducting a successful workshop takes knowledge, skill, experience, careful preparation, and attention to detail. The workshop leader's checklist that follows is designed to help workshop leaders attend to the details. Facilitators must be sure the program advertised is what they plan to deliver, that the room is set up as requested, and that workshop evaluations are appropriate. These factors contribute to successful workshops, and no one can afford to assume that everything will be taken care of.

Workshop Leader's Checklist

In preparation for a successful workshop, these are the items to check and the questions to ask:

Promotion, advertising
What is my role?
Is the session advertised clearly and accurately?
Will it stimulate interest?
Can I deliver exactly what the advertisement says I will?

Objectives
What is the theme of the session?

What will participants gain?
What exactly is to be achieved?
Are objectives reasonable, achievable, flexible?

Agenda
Is it clear?
Is adequate time allowed for each item?
Have I included:
Introductions
Warm-up
Business
Activities
Discussion
Wrap-up

Physical environment
What is the location?
Has it been booked?
Is the space adequate and comfortable?
How will the furniture be arranged?
Who will arrange the furniture?

Introductions
Will someone introduce me?
If yes, what do I want them to say?
Do participants need to introduce themselves?
Will we want nametags? Who will provide them?

Learning activities
Is this the best way to achieve the objectives?
Is the time adequate?
Will participants enjoy themselves?

Learning aids
What props do I need?
chalkboard
Video
Overhead
Tape recorder
Microphone
Lectern
Flipchart
Projector
Film

Other materials
Coffee
Water
Paper

Pencils
Handouts

Evaluation
Did the session meet its objectives?
Is the participant evaluation clear and simple?

☐ How to Generate Energy

It seems useful to talk about a good experience as one that gives energy and a bad experience as one that robs people of energy. Many retired people talk about having less energy to draw on than they used to have and certainly any kind of illness or disability is a drain on one's energy reserves. As people grow older, the need to have the energy to do the things they want becomes increasingly important.

Individually, people are turned on, motivated, or energized by different things. A few are so self-motivated that they will sit through anything that relates to their personal interests; others catch the enthusiasm that a good facilitator projects; others are energized by new ideas or ideas they can translate into action.

A good workshop presentation will include

• Enthusiasm on the part of the facilitator
• Presentation and stimulation of new ideas
• Practical application of new ideas to the lives of participants

A skilled workshop leader will do all of this and something more. One of the greatest gifts a skilled workshop leader can give is that extra shot of energy that goes beyond motivating people individually. When the workshop leader develops a well-functioning group, people suddenly find energy they never knew they had. McCay (1973) observed,

> People often go to parties, reunions, bars, locker rooms and church services in search of shared good feelings. To the degree they are able to rise above or forget their personal ambitions and problems, they experience a rise of energy and spirit from the communion. (p. 21)

Tremendous jumps in both energy and performance can be generated when members commit themselves to developing ideas and creating positive feelings. When the workshop leader creates a caring and supportive atmosphere in which participants share ideas and feelings freely, the participants develop an increasing capacity to understand themselves and the needs of others. And when members of a group all feel needed and valued, they become willing to commit themselves to the group's common goals. Thus, energy is mobilized for both individual growth and group productivity.

☐ Leadership and the Quality of Excellence

The senior leader is a unique volunteer, not just a volunteer who happens to be older. Senior leaders have decades of experience, knowledge, and skill from a great many different working situations and life experiences. They strive for excellence in themselves and promote it in their groups. It is never too late to put the standard of excellence at the top of personal and leadership goals. Leaders who strive for excellence

- Help the group determine its needs
- Act on issues
- Focus on people and learning to understand them
- Encourage all group members to become leaders
- Challenge others to do their best
- Have confidence in the abilities and trustworthiness of others
- Help and support others in new and difficult tasks
- Help the group develop strengths and unity
- Show an appreciation for all people, groups, and cultures
- Are conscious of mental and physical health
- Set goals for themselves and with their groups
- Know that leaders are made, not born, and continually work on developing their skills
- Are flexible and open to new ideas
- Serve the people and empower others to accomplish the task
- Remain calm and efficient under pressure
- Know when others are more skilled than they are and step aside to let them succeed

Excellent leaders are those who can transform intention into reality. They communicate their vision and garner support from others for it. They are passionate, persistent, consistent, and focused, maintaining the group or organization's effectiveness when the going gets rough. They create a dynamic and supportive working environment in which they can harness people's energies to bring about desired results.

In retirement, an excellent leader is not a person who has a following. The leader is a follower in the sense that he or she follows the lead or needs of group members. Leadership is the art of influencing others not to follow but to become involved and to act. Senior volunteers will not abide a style of leadership that controls by reward and punishment or one in which the leader has access to higher levels of authority and wields it over others.

Generally speaking, retired people do not receive a raise for excellence, a better work space, new equipment, lunch with the boss, or a letter of recommendation for bigger and better volunteer jobs. They do need ongoing support and recognition; they do need thank you notes; they do need to be challenged and given increasingly more demanding activities; they do need to be given the authority to do the job; and they do need training opportunities.

The leader's style is the main reason volunteers are involved in developing their own personal, more effective style and sharing better, more efficient, or more creative ideas. If the leader is open, free, creative, enthusiastic, energetic, and positive, coworkers and volunteers are affected. In other words, the leader's style makes the difference. Most organizations and groups have individuals capable of solving problems, creating fresh ideas, and achieving goals in more effective ways. Whether the members feel involved or self-confident enough to share their ideas depends on the leader's style. When leaders establish an encouraging atmosphere in which members can break out of old ways, become creative, and speak their minds, energy will start to flow, people will be happier (because they feel they come first), and the work will be accomplished at a level of astonishing quality.

The leadership styles of the past, based on autocratic, authoritarian wielding of power in which the boss has rigid rules, will not work with senior volunteers. Motivation and encouragement are key to bringing meaning and purpose to the lives of older adults. This style gets people up in the morning and gives them a reason to be involved. This style demonstrates to people that there is something in it for them, and that something is creating healthy, happy volunteers. George Bernard Shaw, in 1905, wrote,

> I am of the opinion that my life belongs to the whole community and, as long as I live, it is my privilege to do for it whatever I can. I want to be thoroughly used up when I die, for the harder I work, the more I live. I rejoice in life for its own sake. Life is not a brief candle to me. It is a sort of splendid torch which I've got to hold up for the moment, and I want to make it burn as brightly as possible before handing it on to future generations. (as cited in Schriesheim & Kerr, 1977, p. 3)

These aspirations are commonly expressed by older adults from all walks of life.

The retirement stage of life may be a period of growth and development of personal potential. Retirees, no less than adults of any age, want and need to feel useful and to have a sense of purpose. This stage characteristically involves the loss of a fulfilling functional role in society, and the task is to create a new, satisfying social role. For many, this may involve assuming leadership roles, perhaps for the first time in their lives.

The relationship between seniors and professionals who work with and serve them is key to the development of individual potential, the creation of new social roles, and the emergence of seniors as leaders and full partners in decision-making processes. Attitudes prevalent in society, reflected in the culture of seniors' groups, about the abilities of older people and their potential contribution to community life are among the strongest forces influencing seniors to become more involved and assume leadership roles in the organizations to which they belong. "The wise leader is not collecting a string of successes. The leader is helping others to find their own successes. Sharing success with others is very successful" (Lau Tzu, as cited in Heider, 1988, p. 161). Leadership skills from earlier life can be transferred to retirement organizations. However, a style that is authoritarian or based on an organizational effectiveness perspective usually needs to be adapted and softened. Learning about the needs and characteristics of retired people, how to listen to them, and how to develop their leadership potential must become the focus. These renewed skills can be developed through effective leadership training: all that is needed is a willingness to change. The same holds true for first-time leaders in retirement. They, too, can benefit from leadership training, but if they lack confidence in a learning situation, it can be a formidable barrier.

Leadership skills of senior volunteers can be put to the greatest use in serving the needs of their organizations by highly skilled and empowering leadership, by organizational leaders who understand how to empower others and who work toward developing a culture of leadership, and by effective education and leadership training that builds skills and confidence, challenges, inspires, and provokes new insights and possibilities. Who is in charge now? No one and everyone. Controlling leaders can learn to share the power. This is built into the word *empowerment* and it is what creates the challenge.

☐ The Final Challenge

The challenge for seniors' organizations is to transform the rhetoric of empowerment into practice, a process occurring around the world. Empowerment does not mean disempowering some people and giving power to others who may not want it and who may lack the knowledge, skills, and attitudes that are needed. Leadership is something that is developed, and it is developed over a lifetime. It is one's life experience and professional training that determines one's style of leadership in retirement. Women who have been in traditional leadership roles in business typically have the same perspective as a man with the same professional background and often have the same style of leadership. Furthermore, although notions of "power with" are drawn from the feminist movement, assuming a feminist perspective on leadership invariably excludes men. Indeed, in Carnegie Hall, Margaret had a history of leadership in business and she was a feminist whose negative attitudes toward men discouraged them from participating. (Louis was the only man on the board and, as secretary, he felt frustrated and powerless in that position.)

A better distinction between power-with and power-over orientations can be made on the basis of language, rather than gender—better because it is more useful. Using a cultural perspective and an approach to research grounded in critical ehtnography, we can identify tradtionally repressive cultures through the dominant discourse and exclusive language associated with a traditional orientation, and we can begin to create a new language associated with a power-with orientation that is more inclusive—a language of possibility that truly empowers people. The language of possibility invites people to share responsibility, gives voice to different perspectives, and supports their development as leaders. As a political vision, it represents a move toward true participatory democracy, one that societies worldwide will embrace.

Empowerment is a process through which people and communities increase their control and mastery of their own lives. For such empowerment to occur, there must be a commitment to providing the needed lifelong education for seniors, not just through sporadic funding opportunities that give seniors a taste of what is possible, only to be frustrated and disillusioned when their creative achievements are inadequately recognized and funding is withdrawn.

What kind of education empowers seniors? What kind of education helps retirees to prepare for a full and productive life in retirement? Education that incorporates the principles of effective adult education and principles of empowering pedagogy, based on an understanding of the characteristics of retired people—the kind of education that stimulates, challenges, and inspires.

Leadership in its truest and purest sense is serving others, discovering people's wants and needs, enabling and motivating them to grow and realize their highest potential. To this end, leaders will create an environment where creativity and innovation flourish, where everyone shares the vision, where everyone has an opportunity to lead, where volunteer activities are an integral part of life, and where people themselves can define their purpose and live their passion. The leadership legacy lives on when those being served grow as persons and become healthier, wiser, freer, more autonomous, and more likely to become leaders themselves. What is left behind is a truly caring community, a community where everyone is important, dignity is upheld, and people are valued. People who feel a deep sense of self-worth will, in turn, encourage other leaders to travel the same path.

A leader who serves group members creates a chain reaction that strengthens as each link is more valued by those on either side and by those at opposing ends. Everyone feels respected and connected, cherished and appreciated. The strong help the weak, the weak help the frail. When each group grows strong, the chain no longer has any weak links. The stronger the parts, the stronger the whole.

Successful leaders provide a sense of connection to the past and a sense of direction toward the future. Their deep belief in the potential of all people, their spirit of enthusiasm, optimism, and confidence in others helps people to create their own purpose. In turn, purpose builds passion, and passion fuels purpose. Leadership in the third age unites both. We have seen this time and again: purpose and passion at work transforming the lives of older adults. It is in helping others rise to excellence, that we do so ourselves.

REFERENCES

Aging Today. (1995, May/June). pp. 4, 7, 9.

Aronowitz, S., & Giroux, H. A. (1991). *Postmodern education.* Minneapolis: University of Minnesota Press.

Atchley, R. C. (1972). *The social forces in later life.* Belmont, CA: Wadsworth.

Atkinson, P. (1990). *The ethnographic imagination.* London: Routledge.

Barth, R. S. (1991). Becoming a community of leaders. In R. S. Barth (Ed.), *Improving schools from within* (pp. 123–146). San Francisco: Jossey-Bass.

Battersby, D. (1989). Ageing and lifelong learning in New Zealand. *Journal of Educational Gerontology, 4* (1), 28–36.

Bell, J. (1992). In search of a discourse on aging: The elderly on television. *The Gerontologist, 3* (3), 305–311.

Bennis, W. (1990). *Why leaders can't lead.* San Francisco: Jossey-Bass.

Bolman, L. G., & Deal, T. E. (1991). *Reframing organizations: Artistry, choice, and leadership.* San Francisco: Jossey-Bass.

Bolman, L. G., & Deal, T. E. (1995). *Leading with soul: An uncommon journey of spirit.* San Francisco: Jossey-Bass.

Bureau of the Census. (1995). *Sixty-five plus in the United States* (Publication No. SB/95–8). U.S. Department of Commerce.

Butler, R. (1975). *Why survive growing old in America.* New York: Harper & Row.

CARP membership tops 300,000. (1997, June). *CARP News,* p. 9.

Carlson, E. (1994). AARP issues blunt warning to panel. *AARP Bulletin, 35* (10).

Chetkow-Yanoov, B. (1986). Leadership among the aged: A study of engagement among third-age professionals in Israel. *Aging and Society, 6,* 55–74.

Chetkow-Yanoov, B. (1995). Continuing leadership among third-age professionals: A way to succussful aging. *Bold 6* (1), 13–17.

Cole, T. R. (1997). What have we "made" of aging? In M. Freedman (Ed.), *Critical issues in aging, no. 1. An Annual Magazine of the American Society on Aging.* (pp. 59, 60). San Francisco: American Society on Aging.

Covey, S. R. (1989). *The seven habits of highly effective people.* New York: Simon & Schuster.

Cox, R. (1987). The rich harvest of Abraham Malsow [Afterword]. In A. Maslow, *Motivation and personality* (pp. 245–271). New York: Harper & Row.

Cross-Durrant, A. (1984). Lifelong education in the writings of John Dewey. *International Journal of Lifelong Education, 3* (2), 115–125.

Cumming, E., & Henry, W. (1961). *Growing old.* New York: Basic Books.

Cusack, S. (1997). *Creating Healthy Community Connections for Isolated elders.* Free paper presented to 1997 World Congress on Gerontology, Adelaide, Australia, August 21.

Cusack, S. A. (1991). Participation with confidence: The development and evaluation of a leadership training program for older adults. *Educational Gerontology, 17* (5), 435–449.

Cusack, S. A., & Thompson, W. J. A. (1992). Leadership training in the third age: The research and evaluation of a leadership and personal development program for the retired. *Journal of Applied Gerontology, 11* (3), 343–360.

Cusack, S. A., Manley-Casimir, M., & Thompson, W. J. A. (1992). *Reconceptualizing leadership in retirement: Problems with the organizational effectiveness model in working with seniors.* Paper presented at the annual conference of the American Educational Research Association. San Francisco. (ERIC Document Reproduction Service No. ED 344 319).

Cusack, S. A., & Thompson, W. J. A. (in press). Mental fitness: Developing a vital aging society. *International Journal of Lifelong Education.*

De Pree, M. (1987). *Leadership is an Art.* MI: Michigan State University Press.

De Pree, M. (1997). *Leading without power:* Finding hope in serving community. San Francisco: Jossey-Bass.

Drucker, P. F. (1994). The age of social transformation. *The Atlantic Monthly, 274* (5), 53–80.

Dychtwald, K. (1994, March 19–21). *The challenge change will bring: Are you ready?.* Address to the 40th annual meeting of the American Society on Aging, San Francisco.

Dychtwald, K. (1997). Wake-up call: The 10 physical, social, spiritual, economic, and political crises the boomers will face as they age in the 21st Century. In M. Freedman (Ed.), *Critical issues in aging, No. 1.* An annual magazine of the American Society on Aging, (pp. 11–13). San Francisco: American Society on Aging.

Eisner, E. (1979). *The educational imagination.* New York: Macmillan.

Fiedler, F. E. (1971). Validation and extension of the contingency model of leadership effectiveness: A review of empirical findings. *Psychological Bulletin, 76,* 128–48.

Friedan, B. (1994). *The fountain of age.* New York: Simon & Schuster.

Gee, E. M., & Gutman, G. M. (Eds.). (1995). *Rethinking retirement.* Vancouver, BC: Gerontology Research Center, Simon Fraser University.

Geertz, C. (1973). *The interpretation of culture.* New York: Basic Books.

Ginsberg, B. (1995). *Trends in older adult education in America.* Seminar address sponsored by the Gerontology Research Center, Simon Fraser University at Harbour Center, Vancouver, B.C.

Glanz, D. (1997). Seniors as researchers in the study of aging: Learning and doing. *The Gerontologist, 37* (6), 823–826.

Grasso, P., & Haber, D. (1995). Leadership training program at a senior center. *Activities, Adaptation and Aging, 20* (2), 13–25.

Gray, J. (1992). *Men are from Mars: Women are from Venus.* New York: Harper Collins.

Greenleaf, R. J. (1977). *Servant leadership.* New York: Paulist Press.

Havighurst, R. J. (1963). Successful aging. In R. H. Williams, C. Tibbits, & W. Donahue (Eds.), *Process of aging* (Vol. I.) New York: Atherton.

Heider, J. (1988). *The tao of leadership.* Toronto: Bantam.

House, R. G. (1973). A path-goal theory of leader effectiveness. In E. A. Fleishman and J. G. Hunt (Eds.). *Current developments in the study of leadership* (pp. 141–147). Carbondale, IL: Southern Illinois University.

Hull, C. L. (1943). *Principles of behavior.* New York, NY: Appleton-Century-Crofts.

Hunt, J. G., & Larson, L. L. (1977, October 27–28). *Leadership: The cutting edge.* Symposium held at Southern Illinois University, Carbondale, IL.

Jarvis, P. (1989). Retirement: An incomplete ritual. *Journal of Educational Gerontology, 4* (2), 79–84.

Josefowitz, N. (1983). *Is this where I was going?* New York: Warner Books, p. 66.

Kaplan, A. (1964) *The conduct of inquiry.* Scranton, OH: Chandler.

Kerschner, H. K. (1994, December). *The white house conference on aging focus group project. Gerontology News,* p. 4.

Klein, A. F. (1970). The anatomy of leadership. *Training for new trends in clubs and centers for older persons.* Ithaca College, Sympmosium conduct ed at Ithaca, NY.

Knowles, M. (1980). *The modern practice of adult education.* Chicago: Association.

Kornfeld, R. (1997, August 19–24). Training the elderly in gerontology and its integration into social support systems. *Empowering senior citizens around the world through education.* Symposium conducted at the 1997 World Congress of Gerontology, Adelaide, Australia.

Kotter, J. P. (1990, May–June). What leaders really do. *Harvard Business Review,* 103–111.

Kreisberg, S. (1992). *Transforming power.* Albany, NY: State University of New York Press.

Krout, J. (1986). Seniors center linkages in the community. *The Gerontologist, 26* (5), 510–515.

Krout, J. (1989). *Senior centers in America.* New York: Greenwood.

Lamdin, L., & Frugate, M. (1997). *Elderlearning: New frontier in an aging society.* American Council on Education. Phoenix, AZ: Oryz.

Laslett, P. (1987). The emergence of the third age. *Ageing and Society, 7,* 133–160.

McCall, M. W., & Lombardo, M. M. (1978). *Leadership, where else do we go?* Durham, NC: Duke University Press.

McCay, J. T. (1970). *Beyond motivation.* New York: Jeffrey Norton.

McClelland, D. C. (1955). *The achievement motive.* New York: Appleton-Century-Crofts.

McClusky, H. Y. (1974). Education for aging: The scope of the field and perspectives for the future. In S. M. Grabowski & D. W. Mason (Eds.), *Learning for aging* (pp. 324–355). Washington, DC: Adult Education Association.

McGregor, D. (1960). *The human side of enterprise.* New York: McGraw-Hill.

Malinowski, B. (1950). *The argonauts of the western Pacific.* New York: Dutton.

Manheimer, R. J., & Snodgrass, D. (1993). New roles and norms for older adults through higher education. *Educational Gerontology, 19* (7), 585–595.

Martin, S. (1990). *The social environment and participation of older people in community programs: A qualitative analysis of three life worlds.* Unpublished master's thesis, Simon Fraser University, Burnaby, Canada.

Martin Matthews, A. & Brown, K. H. (1987). Retirement as a critical life event: The differential experiences of women and men. *Research in Aging, 9,* 548–71.

Maslow, A. H. (1968). *Toward a psychology of being.* New York: Van Nostrand.

Maslow, A. H. (1987). *Motivation and personality.* New York: Harper & Row.

Melcher, A. J. (1977). Leadership models and research approaches. In J. G. Hunt & L. L. Larson (Eds.), *Leadership: The cutting edge* (pp. 84–108). London: Feffer & Simons.

Miles, M. B. & Huberman, A. M. (1984). Drawing valid meaning from qualitative data: Toward a shared craft. *Educational Researcher, 13* (5), 20–30.

Mitchell, B. A., & Gee, E. M. (1996). Young adults returning home: Implications for social policy. In B. Galaway & T. Hudson (Eds.), *Youth in transition to adulthood: Research and policy implications.* (pp. 61–71). Toronto: Thompson Educational Publishing.

Moody, H. R. (1988). *Abundance of life: Human development policies for an aging society.* New York: Columbia University Press.

Morris, R. M., & Bass, S. A. (1986). The elderly a surplus people: Is there a role for higher education? *The Gerontologist, 26* (1), 12–18.

Myers, J. E. (1993). Personal empowerment. *Ageing International, XX* (1), 3;4;6–8.

National Advisory Council, Population Studies Division. (1988). Provincial and international perspectives on senior populations. *Info-Age, 1* (1). Ottawa: Statistics Canada.

Neugarten, B. L. (1977). Personality and aging. In J. E. Birren & K. W. Schaie (Eds.), *Handbook of the psychology of aging.* New York: Van Nostrand Reinhold.

Norman, A. (1987). *Aspects of ageism.* London: Centre for Policy on Aging.

Ogawa, R. T., & Bossert S. T. (1989, March). *Leadership as an organizational quality.* Paper presented at the annual meeting of the American Educational Research Association, San Francisco.

Ott, J. S. (1989). *The organizational culture perspective*. Chicago: Dorsey.

Palmore, E. B. (1990). *Ageism: Negative and positive*. New York: Springer.

Payne, B. P. (1977). The older volunteer: Social role continuity and development. *The Gerontologist, 17* (4), 355–61.

Peters, R. S. (1961). *The concept of motivation*. London: Routledge & Kegan Paul.

Peters, R. S. (1972). Education and the educated man. In R. Dearden, P. Hirst, & R. Peters (Eds.), *Education and the development of reason*. (pp. 3–18). London: Routledge & Kegan Paul.

Peterson, D. A. (1978). Toward a definition of educational gerontology. In R. H. Sherron & D. B. Lumsden (Eds.), *Introduction to educational gerontology*. (pp. X–X). Washinton, DC: Hemisphere.

Postman, N. (1995, May 28–30). *Public education: Meeting the challenges*. Keynote address to the Canadian Teachers' Federation National Conference, Montreal, Quebec, Canada.

Pratt, H. J. (1995). Seniors' organizations and seniors' empowerment: An international perspective. In D. Thurz, C. Nusberg, & J. Prather (Eds.), *Empowering older people: An international approach* (pp. 53–81). Westport, CT: Auburn House.

Retsinas, J. (1995, March/April). Clouds gather over social security. *Aging Today, 1V1* (2), 1.

Schein, E. H. (1985). *Organizational culture and leadership*. San Francisco: Jossey-Bass.

Schriesheim C. A. & Kerr, S. (1977). Theories and measures of leadership: A critical appraisal of current and future directions. In J. G. Hunt & L. L. Larson (Eds.), *Leadership: The cutting edge* (pp. 9–45). London: Feffer & Simons.

Schultz, C. M., & Galbraith, M. W. (1993). Community leadership education for older adults: an exploratory study. *Educational Gerontology 19* (6), 473–488.

Share or suffer. (1995, May 1). *The Province*, p. A18.

Snider, J. C., & Ceridwyn, N. H. (1986). Guide to growth in the gray classroom. In B. C. Courtenay (Ed.), *Helping older adults learn*. Washington, DC: American Association for Adult and Continuing Education.

Speers, L. C. (Ed.) (1995). *Reflections on Leadership*: How Robert K. Greenleaf's theory of servant-leadership influenced today's top management thinkers. New York: Wiley & Sons.

Stogdill, R. M. (1974). *Handbook of leadership: A survey of the literature*. New York: Free Press.

Streib, G. F., & Schneider, S. J. (1971). *Retirement in American society*. Ithaca, NY: Cornell University Press.

Stogdill, R. M. (1974). *Handbook of leadership: A survey of the literature*. New York: Free Press.

Takanyaki, P. (1997). Diversity and compassion: Keys to reaching students. *Aging Today, XVII* (6), 3.

Tannenbaum, R. (1961). *Leadership and organizations: A behavioral science approach*. Toronto: McGraw-Hill.

Thompson, W. J. A., & Cusack, S. A. (1991) *Flying high: A guide to shared leadership in retirement*. Burnaby, Simon Fraser University.

Thurz, D. (1993). The possibilities of empowerment. *Ageing International, XX* (1), 1–2.

Thurz, D., Nusberg, C., & Prather, J. (Eds.). (1995). *Empowering older people: An international approach*. Westport, CT: Auburn House.

Toseland, R. W. (1990). Long-term effectiveness of peer-led and professionally led support groups for caregivers. *Social Service Review, 64* (2), 308–327.

Tournier, P. (1988). Lifestyles leading to physical, mental, and social wellbeing in old age. *Journal of Religion and Aging, 4*, 13–26.

Tyler, R. W. (1960). The contribution of the behavioral sciences to educational research. In F. W. Banghart (Ed.), *First annual phi delta kappan syposium on educational research*.

Veelken, L. (1997, August 19–24). *Learning for volunteer activities in senior studies*. Paper presented at the 1997 World Congress of Gerontology, Adelaide, Australia.

Vitez, M. (1997). Longevity conference examines world problems, solutions. *Aging Today, XVII* (6), 1.

Weber, M. (1947). *The theory of social and economic organization.* Glencoe, IL: Free Press.

White, R. R. (1958). The language of motives. *Mind, 67,* 258–263.

Yukl, G. (1988). *Leadership in organizations.* Englewood Cliffs, NJ: Prentice-Hall.

INDEX

Page numbers followed by an *f* indicate figures; those followed by a *t* indicate tables.